GW01513755

A Tribute to Frederick Fennell

Robert Simon

GIA Publications, Inc.
Chicago

Copyright © 2004 GIA Publications, Inc.

ISBN 1-57999-472-5

G-6532

Printed in the United States of America

GIA Publications, Inc.
7404 S. Mason Ave.
Chicago, IL 60638
1-800-442-1358
www.giamusic.com

ALSO AVAILABLE FROM

GIA PUBLICATIONS
By Robert Simon

Percy Grainger The Pictorial Biography with a Foreword by Frederick Fennell. Hardback—166 pages

This FF volume is dedicated affectionately to my old friend across the sea: John Bird! What great memories staying with you in 1980 — 38 years ago — Wow!! Stay well and wishing you the best on an epic move to a new home.

Take Care Always,
Rob

Fennell

Acknowledgements

- Larry Lee Adair
- William Anderson
- Wayne Asbury
- Ronald Bishop
- Frank Battisti
- John Beck
- John R. Beck
- Dennis Beck
- Elizabeth Dallman Bentley, GIA Publications
- Jane Bent
- Roger Bobo
- Michael Bookspan
- Brain Co. Ltd., Hiroshima, Japan
- James D. Branch
- Susan Branch
- Wayne Brill
- Cmdr. Lewis J. Buckley
- Master Sargeant Kevin Burns
- Penny Buttler
- Leone Buyse
- Lt. Colonel Philip C. "Carl" Chevallard
- The Hon. William J. Clinton, 42nd President of the United States
- David Peter Coppen, Special Collections Librarian, Sibley Library, Eastman School of Music
- Nicholas DeCarbo, Ph. D., Associate Dean, Professor of Music Education and Music Therapy, University of Miami
- William DesChamps
- Chris Donze, President, Ludwig Music Company
- Earle Dhus
- Jonathan D. Elmore, editor
- Janette Erickson
- Michael Faulhaber
- David Fetter
- Wilma Cozart Fine
- Sandy Flesher
- T. Vernon Foster
- Sam Fricano
- Ron Friedman
- George Gaber
- Hyman Gold
- Helen Chelengarian-Greene
- Alec Harris, President GIA Publications
- Cheryl Hawkins, Telarc Records
- Paul Heaton, Interlochen Center for the Arts
- Norman Horowitz
- Mark Humphreys
- Jeanette Dowd Hurlburt
- Judy Johnson
- Cliff Johnson
- Jerry Junkin
- Michael Kaiser, President, Bridget Siedlecki, Manager, John F. Kennedy Center
- Mr. Kawamura, photographer
- William Klinger
- Kosei Publishing, Tokyo, Japan
- Kevin LaVine
- John Lagerquist
- William Lee
- Dr. David Levy
- Dries Linssen
- Bill Ludwig
- Anne Lutz
- Roger Mastroianni, photographer, Cleveland Orchestra
- Max McKee
- Michael Metcalf
- Tom Miller
- Hirofumi Mizuno, director, audiovisual section, Kosei Publishing
- Jerry Moors
- Lt. Col. Gilbert H. Mitchell
- Jon Newsom, Library of Congress
- George Oldziey
- Helen Ouzer, Louis Ouzer estate
- Paul D. Parkman
- Vincent Patterson
- Harvey Phillips
- Gregor Pierce
- Ken Pick
- Nicholas Poccia
- Polygram Records - Universal Recordings (formerly Mercury Records)
- Alfred Reed
- Kevin Reed, Photographer Dallas Wind Symphony
- Gary Reider, Telarc
- Jack Renner
- David Rezits
- Denise Rodio
- Jim Rohner, Publisher, The Instrumentalist
- Denisse A. Santo
- Albert Saurini
- Loras John Schissel, Library of Congress
- Norman Schweikert
- Steve Seiffert

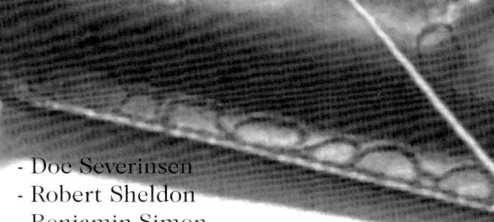

- Doc Severinsen
- Robert Sheldon
- Benjamin Simon
- Jacob Simon
- Sarah Simon
- William Simon
- Joan Templar Smith
- Melvin Stecher
- Tammy Sun
- Tokyo Kosei Wind Orchestra
- Michael J. Wagner
- David Weisbrot, Universal Music
- John Whitney
- Sir David Whitwell
- Robert Woods
- James Undercoffer

Book Jacket and Publication Design by:
Visual Viewpoint
R. Darron Walsh, Principal

Table of Contents

	page
Introduction	7
From the Top	13
Interlochen Letters	33
Eastman Letters	43
Miami Letters	101
FF Impressions	109
Military Bands	163
Celebrating Fennell at 90, an Appreciation by Loras John Schissel	202
Fennell Letters	207
Autobiographical Writing, Frederick Fennell: Lifetime Listener	222
Honors and Awards of FF	236
Index	238

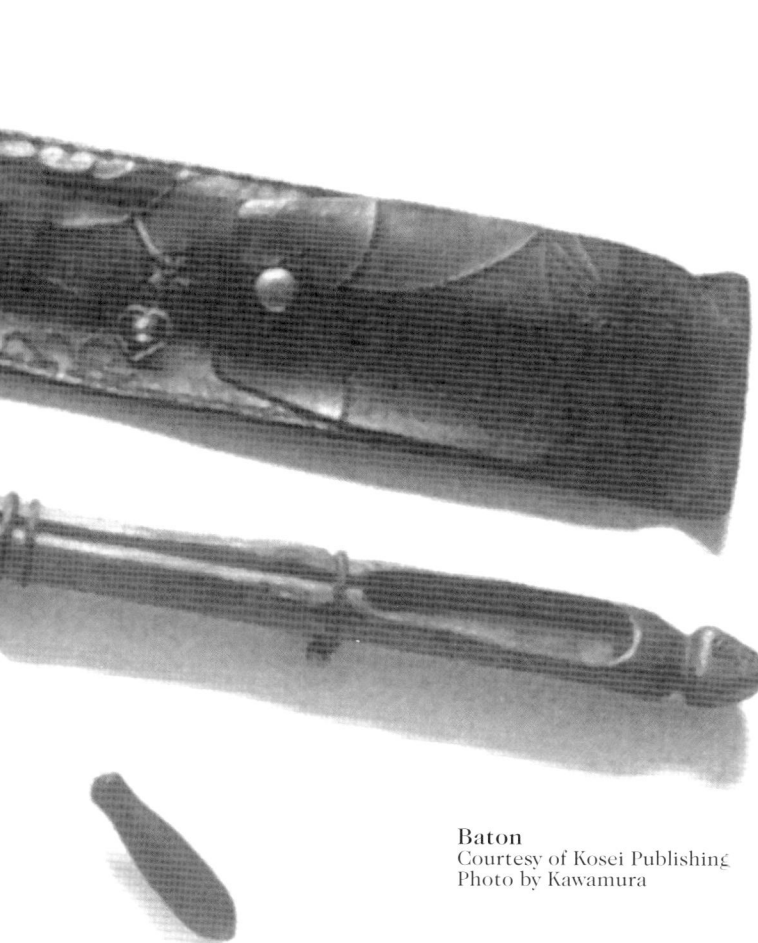

Baton
Courtesy of Kosei Publishing
Photo by Kawamura

Photo by Kawamura—Courtesy of Kosei Publishing.

Introduction

My first encounter with Frederick Fennell was through a fortunate reissue of the British Band Classics (Holst, Vaughan Williams, Grainger) recording on the Mercury Golden Imports label that I purchased in the ninth grade. The vibrant Eastman Wind Ensemble covers and Frederick Fennell's jacket notes sandwiched the vinyl of the most appetizing and incredible sounds I had ever heard. It was the distinctive sound of *Hill Song No. 2* coupled with the program notes that created my interest in Percy Aldridge Grainger.

The recording was suggested to me by my private trumpet teacher, and soon to be high school band director, Max Gonano, who thankfully switched me to playing tuba. This pleased my current band director, John Hamilton, and proved to be a move that changed the direction of my life. To demonstrate how musical and vital the tuba was, Max played me the introduction of the Holst *First Suite* from that Eastman recording. I had to have it! I mowed lawns, worked for my mom and bussed tables to buy every recording Fennell had available. To say the least, I was motivated. I still cherish those records today, even though the grooves are worn out. (Fortunately, they have been reissued on compact discs.)

I loved playing the tuba, and the next season found me in the high school marching band with an ex-military brass sousaphone wrapped around me. During a football game, we were playing our fight song after scoring a touchdown and a gust of wind blew me off the top bleacher, knocking me out cold. That must have been an indication for the band director to promote me to drum major. For the next two years, I enjoyed the leadership and conducting opportunities that such a position afforded me. I often practiced conducting to some of my coveted Fennell recordings. This led me to pursue a music major at the University of North Carolina at Chapel Hill with a partial scholarship; at UNC, the tuba teacher and wind ensemble conductor, David Reed, was an Eastman graduate.

My interest in Percy Grainger's life and music grew quickly at UNC. Several faculty members and fellow students teased me about my fascination with Grainger because he was an unusual figure and not acknowledged in our twentieth-century course books. A retired professor and renowned musicologist, William S. Newman—who actually knew Grainger in the 1940s—encouraged me to stay the course and pursue my curiosity. I received a summer study grant from the Class of 1938 to further my research on Grainger, and it would send me to the Grainger Museum at the University of Melbourne in Australia.

During this time, Frederick Fennell was recording the first digital recordings with Telarc and writing a series of articles for *The Instrumentalist.* I contacted Fennell to see if I could do any research for him while at the museum. It was the perfect introduction. The Maestro not only loved and recorded Grainger's music but was a dear friend to Percy in his final years. Stewart Manville, the curator of the Grainger Library in White Plains, NY, gave me Fennell's phone number. He picked up the phone on the second ring and answered with that enthusiastic greeting, "Frederick Fennell," a sound that would become familiar over the next twenty-five years.

I introduced myself, explaining about the university grant and how my interest in Grainger started by hearing his recordings while I was in junior high school. He was genuinely excited for me and my project saying, "We must meet – are you coming to the convention?" I said yes, and he gave me a day and time to meet him at the Ludwig Music booth. When I hung up the phone I was beside myself – I just had a great conversation with Frederick Fennell, but I did not know where or when this convention was being held! I went to Ed Bostley, our music education professor and another Eastman graduate, and asked about this convention. I explained that I had agreed to meet Fennell and was too embarrassed to tell him that I did not know about the existence of the convention much less how I would get there. Dr. Bostley said it was in Miami and he would arrange a trip if I would round up a few more students and a university car. The students were easy; however, the car was a different matter. I called carpool and all the vehicles were allocated. Finally, I hustled over to transportation and pressed them for a couple of cars claiming they promised us three cars for this convention. They offered one (which was all we really needed) and off we were in a mighty, Carolina blue Plymouth.

Waiting at the Ludwig booth, I heard that perceptible voice call "Robert" and I turned to meet the Maestro, my idol. I had never seen him before in person; in my mind, was the bold name on the record covers. I have to admit that I expected to meet a tall and suave figure. I glanced down slightly and there was this compact man with a sparkle in his eye, a big smile, and a leather satchel under his arm. He introduced me to his wife, Lynne. Shortly thereafter, we got down to business.

The Maestro explained his conductor's analysis of *Lincolnshire Posy* would be published in *The Instrumentalist* by the fall, and *Hill Song* would follow later. He also said he was working on a full score edition of *Posy* in which all the hundreds of errors would finally be put to rest. He gave me a few things to check (or double check) at the Grainger Museum. Dr. Fennell also put me in contact with Wayne D. Shirley in the music division of the Library of Congress. Shirley was overseeing the U.S. Grainger collection (almost 16,000 items) soon to be sent to the museum in Australia. My research grant ended in a pictorial biography and discography of Percy Grainger, and the foreword was tastefully composed by Frederick Fennell. Currently, my Grainger book is available in its third edition from GIA Publications, Inc., Chicago.

I have so many fantastic memories of the Maestro. While researching at the Library of Congress, I had the treat of watching him rehearse and conduct a series of concerts in Coolidge Auditorium. Three phrases stick in my mind from those rehearsals: "LISTEN," "WAIT," and "IT IS NEVER PLAYED TOO SHORT." Countless times, I have traveled to see him rehearse and perform. To me he is mesmerizing and inspiring. He has guest conducted my groups from time to time. We produced a wonderful live double compact disc with our Piedmont Wind Symphony, and at the end of the *Posy* one can hear him murmur "thank you" to the musicians. I have sat and had score study with him prior to rehearsal. His score study is like a religious meditation. Fennell knows the music and rehearsal numbers even better than the composers may have. He crafts his own hand-bound scores filled with exact markings, anecdotes, photos, and memories of the composers, and, above all, his annotated analyses. His massive collection will eventually be housed in the Library of Congress for all to access.

Imprinted in my mind was my conducting of the *William Byrd Suite* with the Maestro standing in the wings, stage right, watching me and listening to the wind symphony for the duration. I glanced at him during the *Mayden's Song* and his eyes and smile were so encouraging. It was possibly our best performance ever, and as I came off stage to switch with him, he said, "That was an excellent job – what a terrific performance." He went on stage and then took the PWS to a new level. The Maestro later wrote, "The Piedmont was ready to play and play they did. So please give them my thanks once again for our concert and my very best wishes for those ahead."

Thinking back, I have never felt nervous around the Maestro, whether on stage, in a discussion, or while he was cooking eggs for Elizabeth (his third wife) and me. Incidentally, his house is an amazing storehouse of music. It even has a picture of Percy Grainger hanging on the wall, one that I developed and sent to him in 1980. Speaking with the Maestro, even at age ninety, is like talking to a college buddy. Frederick treats everyone like a peer, is engaging in his conversations, and has quite a sense of humor. He continues to be incredibly perceptive, stating, "A concert can no longer just be a concert – it has to be an event."

In 1987 we organized a two day Percy Grainger Music Festival at Salem College in Winston-Salem. Fred was one of the main guests and he conducted a joint choir of the Salem College Chorale, the Converse College Chorale, the Piedmont Chamber Singers and the Winston-Salem Brass Ensemble. I prepared his scores for the choral and brass pieces. While he was rehearsing *I'm Seventeen Come Sunday*, he stopped the choir, turned to me, and said: "There are eight bars missing." Indeed there was a page missing, but we decided he would just compensate for this as the missing page was basically a repeat except for text. So, we just added a repeat sign. As he was further in the piece, he stopped and turned to me again and this time his facial expression had, shall we say, the evil eye. He exclaimed, "Now we're missing sixteen bars!" I flew to the podium feeling a little panic and grabbed the score. I realized Fred had just over-looked a repeat sign as the copy was not clear; he had no advance study time. I leaned over and quietly said (not wanting to appear as if I was correcting him): "This one is a repeat." He looked back at it, smiled, and graciously said to everyone, "This was my mistake – let's do it again."

After college, I told the Maestro I was not pursuing music as a full-time career, and he seemed to respect my decision. We stayed in touch once a year or so, usually discussing Percy Grainger. Before long, I was hired to form a wind ensemble at the North Carolina School of the Arts. The Maestro wrote me from Japan: "Congratulations... this is certain to be a great experience and I wish you all good things with it. Repertory is the name of the game, and while ours is comparatively small, it does have a stable core and the promise of increase. But, if we do not play – and replay what we have, the thrust for it may well disappear."

I have seen the Maestro do, and say, some astonishing things. At an Eastman reunion concert that opened with the *Duke of Marlborough* fanfare, there was an early entrance in the trumpet section, and the Maestro wiggled that powerful left index finger to erase the mistake before it took effect. I often joke that Fred's powerful finger and magical stance influenced Steven Speilberg's concept of E.T. Just before his 87th birthday, while conducting the third movement of the Bennett *Symphonic Songs*, he pulled a slide whistle out of his pocket to cover the part before the coda. After intermission, he came onstage carrying an original nineteenth-century rope tension field drum and played the *White Cockade*, a Civil War Union cadence. It was followed by *Connecticut Half-Time*, but first he warmed up with a technically difficult nine ratamacue (a drum rudiment with an alternating stick pattern). He conducted the concert with John Philip Sousa's baton, the same baton Sousa used to conduct the band at Interlochen Music Camp in which Frederick played the bass drum as a teenager.

Years earlier, I unexpectedly appeared at a rehearsal of the Holst *Hammersmith* with a university group, and the Maestro did not know I was coming. In the beginning of the Scherzo, the piccolo player was stuck, starting on a fictitious downbeat instead of the upbeat as written, and all the musicians followed as though the music was rewritten. He would have none of that and went to task breaking the habit, which took many takes. He turned around, saw me sitting there, raised his hands and said, as if we were the only ones in the hall, "Robert – it's as though I'm speaking to them in Swahili."

Once, during a concert at Coolidge Auditorium after the fourth movement of *Lincolnshire Posy*, the Maestro spontaneously spun around on the podium and bellowed out *Lord Melbourne* in the 1905 style of folksinger George Wray as documented on an Edison wax cylinder recording. Whirling back around into his anacrusis, the ensemble belted out the most resounding Graingeresque *Lord Melbourne* I have ever heard. It was a riveting and transcendental performance.

Between rehearsals at Wake Forest University, a temporary stage extension was set up with some unusual step heights that were not marked with the traditional black and yellow safety stripes. The Maestro was talking to a couple of us and he caught his shin badly on one of the steps and faltered. He got up and said: I'm okay – it is just a scratch." He did a two and a half hour rehearsal and his white pants leg was blood soaked. He never complained.

As a testament to his unwavering energy, for his 90th birthday the maestro conducted the Blossom Festival Band (of the Cleveland Orchestra) on July 3, 2004, during a celebration of Independence Day. It was a gratifying experience to be among the 14,000 fans who sang "Happy Birthday" to the man who has given so much to us for so long.

It is an undisputed fact that Frederick Fennell is one of the greatest links to twentieth-century music history, as evidenced by his work and personal contacts with Koussevitzky, Fürtwangler, Beecham, Copland, Bernstein, Grainger, Vaughan Williams, Stokowski, Toscanini, Stravinsky, Leinsdorf, Hanson, Sousa, Lukas Foss, Morton Gould, Andre Previn, Karl King, Karel Husa, Henry Fillmore, Bernard Rogers, Robert Russell Bennett, Alec Wilder, Vincent Persichetti, John Krance, Paul Whiteman, Leroy Anderson, William Schuman, and the list goes on for pages. He has created the modern-day wind ensemble but is not limited to the band. He has conducted the Boston Pops, the London, Minneapolis, Houston, and Miami Symphony Orchestras, and countless operas and has recorded and performed relentlessly around the world. Frederick Fennell has produced hundreds of recordings and conducted thousands of performances, touching the lives of millions.

I know my story and thoughts are not unusual. Frederick Fennell has been there encouraging thousands of musicians for decades. He has been here almost a century and has seen and done it all. What an impact that first recording of the Eastman Wind Ensemble and the program notes made on my life as a musician! For those who have never heard the Maestro speak, he talks in a precise warm cadence to accentuate his point. I will always hear his voice in my head, saying "keep on doing what you do."

Robert Simon
Summer 2004
e-mail: RSmaestro@aol.com

Holst, Vaughan Williams and Percy Aldridge Grainger.
–For Simon, this was the beginning.
Courtesy of Universal Polygram Records.

WASBE Performance "Arigatou."
Courtesy of Kosei Publishing, photo by Kazamura, 1995.

From the Top

Frederick Fennell is an authentic musical force, a conductor of high energy and deep perception. Along with his unmatched skill and experience, Fennell's extraordinary personality enables him to achieve astonishing performances of unique precision and clarity; he treats every musical nuance as though it were a precious gem. A musical genius and scholar, the Maestro inspires countless musicians from the podium, through his groundbreaking recordings and publications, and through direct personal contact.

Frederick Fennell developed the twentieth-century wind ensemble and influenced many of its disciples. With the honor of the pioneer comes the duty to put the best original works in constant performance and engender a demand for new compositions, while constantly setting the highest standard of excellence for generations to follow. His pure love of music and its history and his meticulous attention to the smallest detail remain inspiring. The Maestro's efforts are indefatigable and his results superior. Fennell's output is beyond prolific in comparison to many of his contemporaries.

In 1914, Gustav Holst began composing *The Planets*; Ralph Vaughan Williams completed *A London Symphony* (Symphony No. 2) and *The Lark Ascending*; Percy Grainger wrote his original setting of *Colonial Song* for keyboard, moved to New York and started *The Warriors*. In that same year, one of the greatest champions of these three composers, Frederick Fennell, the son of Fred and Julia, was born on July 2 in Cleveland, Ohio. Shortly

Fred's father in 1905 on Chippewa Lake, Ohio. Behind him on the left was his first wife, Julia, Frederick's mother, who died in 1915. Beside her is sister Kathryn who later married father Fred and helped to raise the children. Photo courtesy of FF via Jon Newsom.

after Frederick's birth, his mother died of influenza and his father faced her loss with the newborn Frederick and an older daughter, Marjorie. In a 2001 interview with Jon Newsom, Fennell explained that his "father eventually married, as was the habit in those days, my mother's sister, Kathryn Putnam, the youngest of three girls."[1] Fred, Kathryn, and the children moved into a large home with Uncle Charlie Putnam and several other relatives.

A rich family legacy of American history and music influenced Fennell's early years. Many of the men in the Putnam family held membership in the *Sons of the American Revolution* and were avid Civil War enthusiasts. The family coupled its passion for history with a unique enjoyment of music by forming a family fife and drum corps. The group gave afternoon performances during the summer at a spot on the family property that they called Camp Zeke, which was:

> *An encampment of people living as people lived during the Civil War. Between the five brothers and their cousins and two outsiders, they would have their platoon of twelve. They learned to do everything as a platoon, and they came into camp at certain weekends, and it was very military, so to speak...In addition to all of these other things that they did as a unit, they organized a fife and drum corps.*[1]

Fennell recalled that "it all began with a fife and drum corps, and I think it was first of all because my father was a fifer in that fife and drum corps, and it was such a great drums corps and it was a great sound. That really is what got me into it because I couldn't stay out of it."[2] Seven-year-old Frederick made his debut playing drums in the fife and drum corps on July 4, 1921, during an Independence Day Celebration. Eighty years later to the day, at age eighty-seven, he would conduct the Winds of the Cleveland Orchestra (Blossom Festival Band) for the 2001 July 4th Independence Day Celebration.

As a student at Miles Elementary School, Frederick sang in the class chorus and was a drummer in the beginning orchestra. By the age of ten, he owned his first drum set and was on his way. Inspired by his experiences in the school orchestra, bands and his family's fife and

Frederick, age 7, with father Fred, Camp Zeke in the background, circa 1921. Father Fred made every effort he could afford to take young Frederick to concerts, including the premier of Sousa's Black Horse Troop *in Cleveland with John Philip conducting the band when a team of black military horses "from Troop A rode onto stage and stood behind the band to the tumultuous cheering of all," in 1925. After that, Frederick thought every time a Sousa march was performed horses should appear. A proud day for father Fred was living to see Frederick conduct the Cleveland Orchestra. Photo courtesy of FF via Jon Newsom.*

First photograph of Frederick Fennell on Parade. The occasion was the dedication of a monument in Burton, Ohio. FF is bottom left corner: "the drum, as usual is bigger than I am." To his left is his father playing fife. Photo courtesy of FF via Jon Newsom.

drum corps, the fundamentals of music seemed to come naturally to Frederick.

Fennell attended John Adams High School where he played mallets and kettledrums in the high school orchestra and band; he also performed with numerous community groups. This time exposed him to a great repertory, including Tchaikovsky symphonies, Rossini overtures, and the music of Wagner and Saint-Saëns. Soon he became the Drum Major at John Adams High School, a unique school in that it offered the students the opportunity for intense study of music theory, harmony, orchestration, and formal analysis.

In the summers, Frederick advanced from Camp Zeke to the National Music Camp at Interlochen, Michigan, which he attended on a scholarship. The opportunities there were limitless, leaving Frederick with seminal impressions, lifetime friends, and numerous experiences working with great professionals such as Howard Hanson, Director of the Eastman School of Music, and Albert Austin Harding, Director of the Illinois University Concert Band. Later, in *Time and the Winds*, Fennell writes of the camp and its creation:

Frederick as Drum Major at John Adams High School, 1932. Photo by: Kathryn Fennell

With the assistance of innumerable well-known conductors, educators, philanthropists, and educational foundations, and with their private fortunes, indefatigable energy and devotion, (Joseph) Maddy and (Thaddeus P.) Giddings established the National High School Orchestra and Band Camp in the pine woods at Interlochen, Michigan. From humble beginnings and with continued unselfish assistance from all who came in contact with this incomparable institution, the camp has grown to a sprawling settlement representing a large financial investment in buildings, facilities, and staff.

Frederick in his John Adams High School uniform performance medals on the chest. Photo circa 1932. Photo courtesy of Ludwig Music Company.

John Adams High School Orchestra in 1930. FF is behind the second kettledrum to the left. Orchestra conductor was Amos Wesler. Photo is courtesy of Hyman Gold, principal cellist in the second row, far left.

Rear view of Camp Zeke. The name comes from the namesake of an eagle Frederick's uncle Charlie found. When Zeke died, he was stuffed and mounted in the camp. Photo courtesy of FF via Jon Newsom.

The main tent of Camp Zeke. The supplies include flags, campfire bucket, wash basins, and equipment for camp life. There are even flag storage boxes and a small portable jackass cannon. Photo courtesy of FF via Jon Newsom. Circa, 1926

The 1500 students of all ages who attend its annual eight-week session continue to sustain this institution (now known as the National Music Camp) as one of America's most unique music education achievements. Many of the thousands of students who had their first memorable musical experiences on the stage of Interlochen Bowl have since become intimately associated with America's important musical institutions. Of equal pride to its founders [are] the countless number of campers who, though following other vocations, have taken their place in the important amateur music-making of their respective communities.[3]

A permanent personal attachment developed between Frederick and Interlochen, and it became obvious to all who knew him that he had an innate ability for leadership already evident at such an early age.

At the end of the Great Depression, Frederick graduated from high school. No doubt, money and college were the issues at hand. Through talent, hard work and burgeoning relationships at the Interlochen Music Camp, Frederick received a scholarship to the Eastman School of Music at the University of Rochester. With his background as a high school drum major, Frederick pioneered the first marching band at the University of Rochester, which he directed for 10 years. His actions were quite innovative for the time and extraordinary for a young man of his limited experience. His majors were music theory and percussion, which certainly contributed to his astonishing analytic precision. He studied privately under the percussionist, William G. Street.

During the off-season, Frederick transformed the marching band into a symphonic band. Even then, he displayed an inherent ability for recruiting fine musicians, shaping their talents and forming them into a fresh, high-spirited organization. Frederick's college years were filled with innovative ideas, challenging classes, astounding rehearsals, and marvelous concerts. Apparently, Dr. Howard Hanson, already impressed with young Frederick from their summers at Interlochen, became even more convinced of Fennell's talents upon working with him at the Eastman School. By fostering Frederick's career and supporting his innovations, Dr. Hanson deserves distinction for his role in the development of the modern day wind ensemble. The Eastman School provided the opportunities for Frederick to excel as a student leader.

After graduation, Frederick married a fellow Eastman music student, Dorothy Codner. During the same year, he received a university fellowship to the *Salzburg Mozarteum* in Germany. His studies there were cut short due to Hitler's move on Europe, but not before Frederick had several classes with Wilhelm Fürtwangler and experienced a taste of European conducting.

Frederick, uncle Maurice Putnam, uncle Will Putnam displaying strong family resemblance with the "Family Spirit of '76." This is inside the Fennell house on Miles Avenue. Federick built the doll-house and furnishings in the background for Kathryn. 1932 Photo courtesy of FF.

Interlochen, 1931, father Fred sitting in the stands of the Grove reading the paper. Photo courtesy of FF.

Upon returning to the Eastman School of Music, Frederick pursued a Master's degree in music theory while continuing to conduct university and area ensembles. In the summer of 1942, Frederick found himself studying under Serge Koussevitzky at the Tanglewood sessions in Boston. His classmates were Leonard Bernstein, Lukas Foss, and Walter Hendl. Koussevitzky, the creator of Tanglewood, taught that to be a conductor is to "awaken in us what we are."[4] Koussevitzky had a keen interest in young musicians. He is considered the greatest conductor of both the Russian school and the Boston Symphony Orchestra.

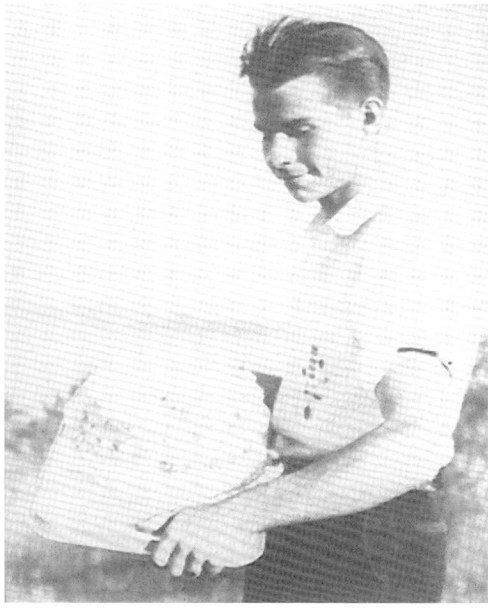

Fred's nineteenth birthday at Interlochen with Cake and gifts from his friends, 1933. Courtesy of Ludwig Music.

During World War II, Frederick served in the USO, working mostly in southern California. He covered areas from San Diego to San Francisco traveling always by car "with gasoline stamps provided."[5] Happy and content with his duties, Frederick outfitted Navy vessels with bands working within specified military guidelines.

After the war, Frederick remarked on a dramatic difference in the attitudes of students at Eastman. He noted that students studying on the G.I. Bill who had played in the military band during the war were "independent in thinking and independent financially."[6] For the next five or six years, Frederick implemented unusual programming and instrumentation, revolutionizing the old-style, big symphonic band. His guest conducting increased as he conducted the Boston Pops for Fiedler.

As fate would have it, Frederick contracted hepatitis because his dentist used unsanitized equipment. Quarantined for weeks in the hospital, Frederick had plenty of time to ponder his revolutionary goals for the symphonic band. Later he would say, "There was nothing else for me to do but rest, think, eat, and sleep."[7] Lying there, "calling on the previous twenty years,"[8] Frederick analyzed the current state of his symphonic band and considered its future. For many years, he had thought of scaling the band down with smaller instrumentation similar to the wind section of the symphony orchestra (plus saxophones and euphoniums). He thereby eliminated the excessive duplication of a typical 100-piece concert band in which clarity and good intonation are rare and many musicians spend their time merely blowing to cancel other musicians out.

Frederick with his drum set, including two Chinese cymbals, toms and bass drum, 1933. Photo courtesy of FF.

FF's debut as conductor with the National High School Band in Chicago, IL, August 19, 1933. Photo courtesy of Barbara Booe.

Discussing the evolution of his thoughts with Jon Newsom, he would say:

Well, as in so many laboratory experiments that people in medicine and various other sciences carry on for many, many years, keeping, you know, records of certain things that happen when you mix certain materials together, it went on for years and years, this experimentation, everybody learning something from it. Mine was a twenty-year learning process…it really did start about my last year at Interlochen. We were walking back to the boy's camp lake (as I mentioned earlier, they had two different lakes) after the Monday rehearsals, which were: first, the orchestra and then the band. Walking through the woods, it so happened that the fellow I was walking with was the superb trumpet and cornet player, Sidney Mear, and I said to him, 'How did it feel to you this morning at the first rehearsal of the orchestra that you were selected the principal trumpet player of the orchestra and then, this afternoon when you sat down in the band, you had your cornet out instead of your trumpet and you were the principal cornet player? Did it sort of make you feel that you're ready to arrive in that field as a professional?' And he said, 'Well, it was very interesting,' (they always had these kinds of auditions before they had the Friday tryouts). He said, 'I enjoyed the orchestra of course. I enjoyed the big band,' (it was a very big band, and Dr. Harding was certainly a very, very good conductor). I didn't say anything. We walked along a little more and then he stopped and said, 'There's only one thing I'll say. In the band, anytime I wanted to put my horn down I could hear ten other guys playing my part.' That's all he said. I didn't have anything to counter it with, but the words stuck with me.[9]

Frederick tuning the timpani at Interlochen, 1933. Photo courtesy Bill Ludwig.

Organizing all these memories and theories was about all Frederick could do in the hospital:

> *You just have to lie there quietly in bed and do nothing and follow, very carefully, the diet they prescribe for you: pass a certain amount of water every hour; drink this and eat raw sugar, all those things that they felt worked on the liver to save it. That was the whole point. And I looked up at the ceiling just about as long as I could look up at it. Not to do anything, but, you know, quiet philosophy, looking up at the ceiling and letting your mind do what you'd like to have it do. That wasn't necessarily a part of life in the Eastman School! (laughs) We were rather busy every day doing everything you could just to stay alive. But I started looking up there at the ceiling saying to myself, well, why don't you take this rare opportunity to try to think through The Eastman Wind Ensemble from the beginning, which I did. And Oscar Zimmerman, the principal bass player and teacher, good friend, came to see me one afternoon. I gabbed to him about this and he says: "Why don't you write it down before you forget about it." And so, I asked my wife to bring me a pad of paper and a pen, and I scratched it all down, and I made a diagram of how they might sit, and I even wrote down about thirty titles I thought we ought to consider playing, all original. And right back in the corner of this thing, I wrote in a box that I had squared off, why not try to make some records? And that was all I ever said about records."*[10]

While still in the hospital bed, Frederick generated detailed notes of his plans and reviewed them with Howard Hanson. Ever supportive of Fredrick, Dr. Hanson approved a trial wind ensemble as soon as Frederick recovered. Frederick knew he had a great opportunity in hand, and from the beginning, he graciously wrote about the vision of the great founders of the musical development in America:

San Diego Symphony at Ford Bowl in Balboa Park. "My first and only professional engagement as a kettle drummer." Photo courtesy of FF.

Photo of Frederick in the study of Betsy Ross cabin on the Putnam farm in 1933. Photo on desk includes Bill Ludwig and his father. FF first heard the National High School Orchestra of Interlochen on this Philco radio. Photo courtesy of FF.

As this base of support for our manifold musical enterprises continues to expand, we find the people in their ever generous way, contributing to the support of a vast musical activity – one, perhaps, of which Thomas Jefferson, Lowell Mason, Theodore Thomas, George Eastman, and others had more than a vision. The institutions that these men toiled to create continue to sustain the faith which was theirs. Among these institutions, and of the utmost importance to the development of the great American musical renaissance, are the schools and conservatories of music which were established by them and others out of their work, their love of the people, and their faith in the art of music. This was a work for men of vision. George Eastman was this kind of man.

In the institution which he founded, it has been possible for Howard Hanson, another such man, to bring the development of the academic and creative aspects of musical education to new heights... The Eastman School of Music with which his life and name are synonymous has been particularly associated with the fields of composition, education, and instrumental performance, although the scope of its influence upon almost every aspect of the art of music is not limited to these three important endeavors. It seems natural, therefore, that this institution should have undertaken the fashioning of what may become another important instrumental development – The Wind Ensemble."[11]

For Frederick, there were no short cuts, no evasions, and everything he did led to higher standards at Eastman and eventually around the world. Frederick recalled the remarkable beginning of the Eastman Wind Ensemble:

We had our first rehearsal on the 20th of September, 1952. Everybody whom I had chosen to play in the group, rather knew that we had a different idea because I chose the best students in the school, and the best solo performers, and the best ensemble players. I gave them responsibility; I gave them pleasure and the joy that playing in a good group can give. And from the beginning they knew that it was up to them to make it into the group that, obviously, I had thought it could be, or I wouldn't have assembled it in the first place. And that repertory, that list of players that I posted on the bulletin board there in the hall of the Eastman School, that's where it all began."[12]

FF in Freshman Class photo.

*Robert Weiss, Pres., Marion Alt, V. Pres., Fred Fennell, Treas.
Absent: Charlotte Rounds, Sec.*

FRESHMAN CLASS OFFICERS

HISTORY

Card board signs, lipstick red question marks, green hair ribbons, skull caps, peanuts and apples were the means by which the freshman class of September 1933 was first known. Since that first week of hilarious embarrassment, it has played its part of the program at the school very well under the able leadership of President Robert Weiss.

Its one special affair which was a dance given in December must surely be praised by any one who attended. Both of the student orchestral organizations have as their members, pupils of his class; and much of the talent in the voice department is lent by its younger members.

With such a history as this in but a few months, how can such a class help but be renowned by the end of a sojourn of four years in the Eastman School of Music?

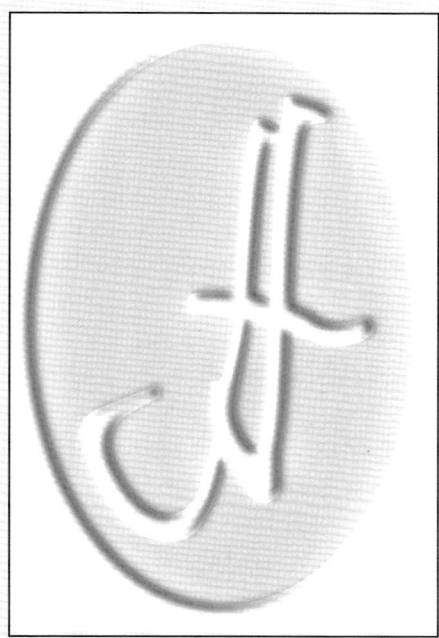
FF has officially arrived.

FF and the University of Rochester Symphony Band, 1936. Photo courtesy of Eastman School of Music.

Frederick also faced the task of finding the repertory for this new ensemble:

> *I had the marching band and the Eastman School Symphonic Band for twenty years, and during those twenty years what programs we played, in spite of my utter failure to get any member of the faculty of composition to write a piece of music for us. I really struck out completely, including with the director [Hanson], who always talked about the importance of the composer. He talked of how important it was that we have [composers] and that they compose their own kind of music for us...It took me twenty years to work it out, twenty years to play everything I could play that was original, rehearse it, and perform it. We even performed some of it on the radio, because the Eastman School had frequent broadcasts at that time. But I had the chance to study it. And I made connections with various men in the principal publishing houses and said to them, "If you have something coming out that's going to be unusual please let me know about it because if I'm just waiting to hear somebody tell me about it, I'd rather have it from you." Well, that's the kind of relationship I built with men who were the representatives of the leading houses, and so we played just about everything you could lay your hands on.* [9]

Fennell (far left, holding pipe) and associates at the Mozarteum in Salzburg, 1938. 1986, The Instrumentalist Co. reprinted with permisson.

Frederick sent letters to approximately four hundred composers around the world, describing his Eastman Wind Ensemble and requesting lists of their appropriate pieces. In addition, he petitioned for new and original compositions for the Eastman Wind Ensemble:

> *My letter stated, in part, that it was our hope that composers would look upon this instrumental establishment as the basic instrumentation from which they could deviate should a particular score require more or less instruments than were listed. It was further stated that they might consider this in the same manner as one does the tutti orchestra, the full organ, or the complete seven-plus octave range of the piano keyboard – a sonority to be utilized only when desired. My correspondents were informed that the Eastman School would have one annual symposium for the reading of all new music written for the Wind Ensemble, and that there would be no "commissions" save those of a performance that was prepared with skill and devotion.*[13]

The first composer to respond was Percy Grainger who was followed by Vincent Persichetti, Ralph Vaughan Williams, and many others. The enthusiasm and momentum catapulted the Eastman Wind Ensemble to the forefront of the musical scene by the mid 1950s. There were numerous concerts, radio broadcasts, and early recording contracts with Mercury Records, resulting in twenty-three records produced in just over a decade. Frederick's Civil War recordings with the Eastman Wind Ensemble, which earned a Grammy Award for music and gunfire in 1961, were a most natural progression from the Putnam family experiences of his childhood. The award was received by C. Robert Fine.[14]

In a letter to Percy Grainger dated July 8, 1952—Grainger's 70th birthday—Frederick wrote about his insight into the potential of the wind ensemble versus the stereotypical perception of the concert band:

> *I sincerely wish that my colleagues would give the Wind Ensemble a whirl. I know it will be a success here, and it could be so in any city in America. I must also be frank to say that I am banking quite heavily on simple terminology. The word "band" is death to too many people. So they are blind and stupid and narrow and prejudiced. Well, I can't say that those who conduct most bands have been able to do much to alter those opinions. But I do not think there are many people who would doubt the success that would attend the following fictional illustration:*

Frederick Fennell came to the University of Rochester six years ago from Cleveland, Ohio. In his Freshman year, he organized the football band that has by this time grown into an organization which commands national attention. The following year, the concert organization was formed as an outgrowth of the marching band. Since then it has grown in size to the point that its unusually full instrumentation has inspired many of the great contemporary composers to score for band. Each year a large number of first performances are included in its concert series as well as its NBC broadcasts which have become annual presentations of the University. THE SCORE salutes the marching organization, that Mr. Fennell has built up, in its football section.

◄······ *Frederick Fennell and the University of Rochester Marching Band 1939 year book, The Score. Courtesy of the Eastman School.*

"The New York Times announced today a projected series of six concerts of music for wind instruments to be played in Town Hall by the wind-brass-percussion section of the New York Philharmonic Symphony Orchestra under the direction of its conductor, Dmitri Mitropolous. Music by Monteverdi, Josquin des Pres, Vivaldi, Mozart, Strauss, Stravinsky, Grainger, Berg, Schoenberg, Toch, Kienek, Schuman, Hindemith, and Mennin will be played on the first Tuesday of the month beginning in September. Concerts are open to subscription by the public." I am certain they would be sold out. But I am equally convinced that if the announcement said that Mitropolous was organizing a band, that people who think it strange and unorthodox (even for Mitropolous!) and would stay away in droves. I wish Mitropolous would try it! But regardless of others, I want to see this idea get a proper development here. We have every facility with which to create and maintain it. We must not fail.[15]

Frederick Fennell is one of the most recorded American conductors in history. His recordings, from monaural and stereo to the forerunners of high-definition recording that pioneered the industry's first digital symphonic recordings, justify a lengthy book in themselves. "Stereo Review" selected his high-definition recording of Percy Grainger's *Lincolnshire Posy* (Mercury, 1958) with the Eastman Wind Ensemble as one of "the Fifty Best Recordings of the Centenary of the Phonograph: 1877–1977." The repertory from the Maestro's magnificent recordings profoundly influenced generations of musicians, conductors, and composers across the globe. These recordings of original pieces from such well-known composers as Gabrieli, Mozart, Hindemith, and Stravinsky spurred other composers to write new works for the wind ensemble. Frederick realized the patriotic importance of documenting American music, from the Revolutionary and Civil Wars, on original instruments, to the marches of John Philip Sousa and popular pieces by George Gershwin and Cole Porter. Composers such as Holst, Vaughan Williams, Grainger, Persichetti, Gould, Bennett, Schuman, Hartley, Jacob, Milhaud, Anderson, Schoenberg, Mennin, Reed, Rogers, and others soared to unexpected heights in this medium due to the force of Frederick Fennell and the Eastman Wind Ensemble.

Leblanc Publications published Frederick's book *Time and the Winds* (1954), which covers the history and development of the wind instruments from Gabrieli through Beethoven, Brahms, and Wagner, to the Eastman Wind Ensemble. *Time and the Winds* is still a standard text on the heritage of wind instruments, ensembles, and bands.

Frederick's concerts, recordings, guest conducting and international tours continued to flourish; however, in 1962, after a thirty-year association with the Eastman School of Music, he resigned to become the Associate Music Director of the Minneapolis Symphony. Though this alliance lasted only two years, the move to Minneapolis may have been a blessing in disguise. Perhaps if the Maestro had remained at the Eastman School permanently, he might have accepted a more administrative role that, no doubt, would have interfered with him doing what he does best—conducting, performing, recording and writing. Moving to Minneapolis was a necessary transition from Eastman, one which opened the door to Frederick's next opportunity.

Shortly after Minneapolis, William Lee, Dean of the School of Music at the University of Miami at Coral Gables, asked the Maestro to conduct the orchestra, start a wind ensemble, and help recruit a distinguished faculty. During his tenure at the University, the program flourished while his personal life underwent several changes. Frederick and Dorothy divorced, and he married a graduate student, Lynne Doherty. Their marriage ended a decade later. He also experienced financial misfortune; he invested in a nightclub that required great effort and unfortunately produced even greater losses.

Frederick returned his focus to guest conducting, master classes, professional recording, and writing a series of essays on the literature for which he was known. During 1977, the Maestro made the recording annals once again when Telarc Records put him on the podium in front of the wind section of the Cleveland Orchestra to produce the first digital symphonic recording in history. From then on, the recordings were magical. Digital sound was no longer a thing of the future; it had arrived and captured the Maestro at his best. The next recording of significance would be with the London Symphony Orchestra featuring Doc Severinsen on trumpet.

About this same time, the Maestro started writing a voluminous series of his repertory analyses, probably his most important and detailed writings, which *The Instrumentalist* published throughout the late 1980s. Upon retiring from the University of Miami as Professor Emeritus, Fennell was promptly recruited by the Catholic University of America School of Music in Washington, DC. In addition to teaching, he conducted the orchestra and wind ensemble. The summers found him at Interlochen and periodically conducting military groups at the Library of Congress in Coolidge Auditorium. His itinerary was constantly full with guest conducting appearances, master classes, and recording sessions. His writings and music editions became a career of their own and continued to intensify. After Fennell conducted at the Vienna Festival, the Tokyo Kosei Wind Orchestra invited the Maestro to guest conduct in Japan.

Maestro Fennell was an immediate success in Japan, and the Tokyo Kosei Wind Orchestra promptly asked him to become their principal conductor. He made Herculean efforts as a globetrotter, to maintain his momentum in the United States while becoming one of the most admired conductors in Japan. The TOKWO was well-endowed, and its performing resources seemed limitless. The Maestro could not speak a word of Japanese when he began his relationship with the TOKWO; however, together they demonstrated music to be a truly universal language: "…Magnificent playing, hot spirits, incredible personal and ensemble discipline, warm and appreciative communication in the rehearsal where technique took the place of language."[17] It is difficult to imagine after his amazing achievements and innovations at Eastman that Maestro Fennell could continue to break barriers.

In Japan, the Maestro was treated almost as royalty. His legendary reputation promoted much needed validation and world recognition for the professional Japanese wind movement. His devotion brought forth a level of excellence that again shook the music world. His association with TOKWO gave the Maestro another opportunity to fulfill one of his greatest dreams: recording all of the major wind repertory. However, his ambitions were not without anxiety:

> *The wind band's repertory is so desperately in need of first-class recording…that I'm getting a little bit concerned that time is going to pass by and I'm not going to get it all done. That has nothing whatsoever to do with ego. That's just the frightening fact that nobody else is doing it, and it's not going to get done, and that's very sad.*[18]

He recorded twenty-eight CDs with the TOKWO. Before the Maestro finished his sixteenth year with the TOKWO, he became the principal guest conductor of the Dallas Wind Symphony, producing five new recordings in Texas.

Two of the Maestro's greatest honors were the building, dedication, and naming of Frederick Fennell Hall in Kofu, Japan by Tokio Kikushima in 1992 and being named the Laureate Conductor of the TOKWO: "No matter what, I go when they call me to conduct. It is the greatest honor. You know, it is the only group of its kind in the world."[19]

In the midst of this whirlwind international career, Frederick married Elizabeth Ludwig, a long-time friend from high school and the President of Ludwig Music Publishing Company in Cleveland, Ohio. A woman of great distinction and a major success in her field, Elizabeth was the first American woman and the first music publisher of any nation to be knighted by the King of Cambodia[20] for achievements in Literature, Arts, and Culture.

Nearly constant companions, the world-traveling couple maintains Elizabeth's home and business in Cleveland and Frederick's home in Siesta Key, Florida. Together they have produced several editions of major works, starting with a full score issue of Percy Grainger's *Lincolnshire Posy* and an astonishing transcription of Stravinsky's *The Firebird Suite*.

The new century finds the Maestro actively guest conducting around the world. His consistently sensitive and perceptive approach to leadership is perhaps the Maestro's greatest gift. Throughout his illustrious

Frederick Fennell posed in 1940. Courtesy of the Eastman School of Music. Photo courtesy of Josef Schiff.

Growing as a conductor included a position directing Interlochen's National High School Band, 1940. © 1987, The Instrumentalist Co., reprinted with permission.

Interlochen Bowl, 1941 with Paul Whiteman (his band played with the National High School Orchestra) to the left and Joseph Maddy, center. Photo by Dorothy Fennell courtesy of Ludwig Music Co.

FF with an Eastman Chamber Orchestra circa 1940s in Kilburn Hall. Photo courtesy of The Eastman School.

career, he has demonstrated unwavering dedication to the advancement of wind music and its performance. His commitment to the Interlochen Center for the Arts, the founding of the Eastman Wind Ensemble, his association with the University of Miami and the Cleveland Winds, and his time with the Tokyo Kosei Wind Orchestra, as well as his countless appearances, essays, music editions, and recordings bear witness to his ever buoyant enthusiasm. Frederick Fennell is undoubtedly the greatest link to twentieth-century wind music, composers, outstanding performances, and recordings. He always creates time to show genuine interest and encouragement to all musicians, especially students, as the personal testimonies and anecdotes that follow will attest.

Notes

1. Newsom, Jon. *Interview with Frederick Fennell at the Library of Congress*, May 2001.
2. Ibid.
3. Fennell, Frederick. *Time and the Winds*. Leblanc Publications, 1954, page 48.
4. Fennell, Frederick. Quote made to the author during an interview on July 5, 2001.
5. Ibid.
6. Ibid.
7. Ibid.
8. Ibid.
9. Newsom.
10. Ibid.
11. Fennell, page 51.
12. Newsom.
13. Hunsberger, Donald. "The Wind Ensemble Concept" from *The Wind Ensemble and its Repertoire*. University of Rochester Press, 1994, page 7.
14. Fennell, Frederick. Quote made to the author during an interview on July 5, 2001.
15. Battisti, Frank. *The Twentieth Century American Wind Band/Ensemble*. Meredith Music Publishers, 1995. Percy Grainger, page 17.
16. Rickson, Roger. *Fortissimo*. Ludwig Music Publishing Company, Inc., 1993, page 287.
17. Ibid.
18. Fanfare. Interview, September 1988, 12-1.
19. Fennell, Frederick. Quote made to the author during an interview on July 5, 2001.
20. Rehrig, William H. *The Heritage Encyclopedia of Band Music*. Edited Paul E. Bierley. Integrity Press, 1966, page 265.

Interlochen Letters

FF during an Eastman rehearsal, circa 1940s.
Photo courtesy of Edward Pettengill.

William F. Ludwig, Jr.

In the summer of 1933, I was enrolled in the prestigious National Music Camp at Interlochen, Michigan. The country is beautiful up there with many lakes and fragrant pines bending in the breezes. The camp was artfully located between two lakes. The performing stage outdoors was constructed using huge tree trunks from the forest and opened onto a vast, open-air auditorium. All performances of the high school band and orchestra took place at this location. After settling into my assigned cabin, I reported to the auditorium for the first orchestra rehearsal. There I met the members of the percussion section and awaited assignment. The piece on the music stand was strange to me. It was Tchaikovsky's *Fifth Symphony*, and I had never heard of either Tchaikovsky or his Fifth Symphony. One of the older percussionists, who introduced himself to me as Fred Fennell, was a repeat camper. He took charge of the section by stepping behind the pair of balanced-action Ludwig & Ludwig timpani and played the entire symphony straight through on only two timpani—a part written for four drums. It was the most amazing thing I had ever seen or heard. Fennell played through the entire symphony without missing a note or being out of tune. By ten that morning, I knew I wasn't so hot as a timpanist.

Fred and lifelong friend Bill Ludwig at Interlochen, 1932. Taken by Mrs. Rhadanes Angelucci. Courtesy of Bill Ludwig.

At Elkhart the most difficult pieces we played were *The Merry Wives of Windsor*, *The Poet and Peasant Overture*, and *William Tell*. These were all two-timpani parts, which were not nearly as complicated as Tchaikovsky's *Fifth Symphony*. I knew I had met more than my match in the brilliant, young Frederick Fennell. I also knew that I would spend the rest of the summer in awe of his mighty prowess. It was a great awakening, but that's what music camps are all about: the chance to see the best talent in the nation. I studied Fennell's every move, and the few times I got a shot at it, I tried to play up to his level. Mostly I spent eight weeks playing bass drum and snare drum in both band and orchestra, because there was no question who was boss—it was Fennell.

He was a kind and patient teacher who helped smooth over the shock that I wasn't the greatest percussionist in the world. In addition, we had a percussion coach from the Cleveland Symphony Orchestra. The CSO's Frank Tichy schooled me with weekly lessons on the percussion parts we were playing in both band and orchestra. In both these organizations, we enjoyed the wonderful exposure to guest conductors of national recognition who made us play above our heads.

Bill Ludwig
Lifelong friend
Ludwig Drum Company

Kenneth L. Neidig

I first became aware of Frederick Fennell when I was in college (1948-52); and my professional respect for him grew tremendously during 15 years as a school band director in Kentucky. Being editor of *The Instrumentalist* (1970-84) provided direct contact with this innovative leader, as we worked together on important publishing projects. From many memories, I have chosen just a few for this book. All have a connection with Interlochen, Michigan (National Music Camp and Arts Academy) very near Traverse City, where I moved to start my own magazine (*BAND*, later called *BDGuide*; 1984-95), when a progressively closer and more personal relationship developed with this short-statured giant of our profession.

Fred had been coming to Interlochen every year for 50 summers, first as a camper and later as a regular guest conductor. I picked him up at the Traverse City airport and as we drove, he described how much the road to camp had changed. As he recalled his very first trip when it was a dirt road at the end of a long journey in a car driven by his father from his home in Cleveland he became more and more excited, actually bouncing nervously in anticipation, apparently reliving feelings now a half-century old but still very much alive!

Conducting a concert in the Eastman Theater in 1943. Photo courtesy of FF.

It was wonderful to share his child-like enthusiasm... and I believe this quality is one of the secrets of his success. I recall many examples through the years, because he was always honestly excited about what he was doing, whether it was a new article, a commissioned work from an important composer, or even the umpteenth rehearsal/performance of a band work that surely was so familiar that he could easily have shifted to automatic pilot.

That same excitement was on display every summer when he and his wife (Elizabeth Ludwig) visited me and my wife (Marianna Gabbi). He played the latest Tokyo tapes for us on my stereo set-up (which he described as a great rig) and especially enjoyed symphony conductor Marianna's knowledgeable comments on the orchestral transcriptions. (You know, of course, that the father of the wind ensemble does love those large band works too!)

One summer he and I were walking through the woods at Interlochen, and Fred pointed out the precise place where the seed for his work with the wind ensemble was planted. He was a student, in the percussion section of the camp's big concert band with doubled instrumentation

Interlochen, June 1st, 1931–After dinner, pass in hand, blue wool sweater around the shoulders, red cap, paddles. This is when I really began to come alive. In the distance the old sawmill that was once a messhall with the cook; house to the right. Those evenings in the canoe interior flat lake never forgotten. I never saw a picture like this of me until this one. I looked okay in my red Jantzen bathing suit, good legs that have held me up on many a podium all these years. — Photo and caption courtesy of FF.

Taken 60 years after the adjacent photograph in the same spot. FF is holding a copy of the 1931 picture. "Age had changed neither the locale nor the person that much." — Quote and photo by Kenneth L. Neidig.

typical of the time. He and another member of the band were walking back to the boy's cabins after rehearsal, and his friend paused on the path and said, "You know I'm one of 10 trumpets in the band, and it really doesn't matter if I play or not. I could lay my instrument down anytime and somebody else will cover the part." The idea germinated over a period of years, nourished by the model of a symphony orchestra wind section, and finally emerged in 1952 at Eastman when Frederick Fennell posted the notice for a new ensemble: one-on-a-part!

I took a picture of him that day on the path through the woods leading to the boy's camp. Age had changed neither the locale nor the person that much. Fred was older, but no less enthusiastic; and as he waved back to me, I saw the scene as a kind of metaphor: an encouragement to follow his leadership, as well as a final good-bye. I put the picture in reserve for the inevitable day it could be used as a cover to accompany an obituary/tribute (editors think that way). I am so glad I never needed it ... in fact, I gave it to him (inscribed with that thought) as a gift for his 80th birthday!

I feel a more valuable tribute is the living legacy we have in the series of study/performance guides he has written on so much of the basic band repertory, and I am proud to have played a part in that process. Again the origin of the idea has an Interlochen connection. It happened during one of those short-but-significant conversations we have all had at an exhibit booth during the MidWest Clinic in Chicago.

Fred was telling me he had advised Joe Maddy to keep a tape recorder on his coffee table and turn it on whenever he was telling a friend about the early days of the world-renowned institution he had created at Interlochen, adding urgency by saying, "You no longer have the luxury of idle conversation." My immediate response was, "May I say the same thing to you? We need to get your knowledge of the great band literature into print." He quickly agreed to start with Holst, and off we went.

Our most recent collaboration came with his foreword for *Rehearsing the Band* (Neidig Services, 1998). In a brief biographical sketch, I noted that Frederick Fennell is recognized as the Dean of American band conductors, and then referred to his formation of the Eastman Wind Ensemble as a concept that spread throughout the profession and placed all serious band conductors forever in his debt.

Happy 90th, Frederick. Thanks for all the professional and personal pleasures you have brought to so many. I especially appreciate your remaining ff on so many important issues during your long and influential career.

Kenneth L. Neidig

Frederick and Dorothy circa 1937. Photo courtesy of the Eastman School of Music Yearbook.

FF with composer Darius Milhaud circa early 1940s. FF recorded his Suite Francaise with the EWE in the 1950s and again in 1989 with the TOKWO. Photo courtesy of the Library of Congress Music Division.

Michael Faulhaber

My memories with Dr. Fennell go back to those wonderful summers at the Interlochen Arts Camp (National Music Camp), 1958-65.

I remember how exciting it was to watch him conduct the High School Band when I was an intermediate. Then, as a high school camper, I had my chance when he would guest conduct the Symphonic Band in the annual American Band Masters concert that we called "Pass the Baton."

However, the best was in 1963 when I was first clarinet in the orchestra. Howard Hanson was to conduct, but Dr. Fennell did the rehearsals, Sibelius #1 and Hanson's Romantic. It was so professional due to his thorough knowledge, and the rehearsals were done without a score! What a fine example he set for the impressionable high school students with that presentation. I'll never forget it, along with my many personal conversations over the years.

God bless Dr. Fennell and all he has done for so many kids at Interlochen. No one loves Interlochen more than he.

Michael Faulhaber
President, American Music Conference
Ward-Brodt Music Company

With wife, Dorothy, on the train platform at New York Central. Taking the train with the Eastman Little Symphony to St Lawrence University. On a cold March 18, 1948. Photo courtesy of FF.

Discussion panel at Lenox Library near Tanglewood. L to R: Leonard Bernstein, Lukas Foss, Aaron Copland, Frederick Fennell, unidentified. From the Koussevitzky Archive at the Library of Congress. Photo by Victor Kraft courtesy of Loras John Schissel at the Library of Congress.

Jeannette Dowd Hurlburt

I performed music under the baton of Frederick Fennell the bicentennial summer of 1976 at Interlochen Arts Camp. Maestro Fennell ignited a spirit and drive within the band collectively and in me individually. Our band performances under Maestro Fennell soared to a higher level than was believed possible. We had so many standing ovations after performing marches under his baton one couldn't count.

With a passion not seen or felt before in a conductor, Maestro Fennell lead our band with the authority and enthusiasm characteristic of a great maestro we had only heard or read about in history. The notes became alive and took on a whole new character when Fennell conducted.

He wasn't a primadona or an uncaring, selfish musician. He cared tremendously. He was patient; he taught us how phrases and accents were meant to be interpreted and to really play *pp* and *ff*. He transformed us so that we all wanted to play only our best under his baton – I sensed his genuis but didn't honestly understand it at that time.

Frederick Fennell transformed me from being a shy, introverted child to one who began to play more passionately and think more passionately about life itself.

He helped me become not just a better musician, but a better human being. After that summer I won the John Philip Sousa Band award while going to a large rather impersonal public high school class in a graduating class of over 500 students. I believe that strong enthusiasm for life has helped shape the better part of my life. Frederick Fennell is a genius who makes me extremely proud to be an American.

Jeannette Dowd Hurlburt
Clarinet

FF at Tally-Ho Music Camp, 1952. Photo courtesy of Michael J. Wagner.

Eastman Letters

*Two portraits by Alexander Leventon. Circa late 1940s.
Photos courtesy of Michael Metcalf.*

Angela Decarne Robinson

My first introduction to Frederick Fennell was during my freshman year at the Eastman School of Music in 1939.

I was a freshman coming from Benjamin Franklin High School in Rochester, NY, where I had been a prominent clarinetist. I now found myself one among many talented and aspiring musicians. What a magical world was opened to many of us by this inspiring teacher and mentor as we participated in the Eastman School Symphony Band under his direction.

His kindness, enthusiasm, skills, and fine musicianship were a living example of what successes could be possible.

I shall remember him as one of many of the Eastman Faculty who made it possible for me to be able to say "Music is my life."

Angela Decarne Robinson
Professor Emeritus of Music
New England College, Henniker, NH

Nicholas Poccia

My first meeting with Frederick Fennell occurred in 1941, the year that I was accepted as a freshman to the Eastman School of Music. I recall my first rehearsal with the Eastman Symphonic Band. The band was so large, and I wondered how such a group could possibly play together and in tune. We did thanks to Fred. My first impression of him was "WOW!" He was such a young conductor, barely older than some of the students. He had a knack for holding the attention of his players. Before attending Eastman, I had the good fortune of playing with a number of professional groups; however, none of the conductors was as dynamic as Fred.

My association with Fennell was not limited to musical activities. I recall spending Sunday afternoons playing softball at a farm on the outskirts of Rochester. Fred Fennell often joined in, and we students got to see another side of our beloved teacher. Fred was a good player, and students made certain that he would leave every game with at least one hit. Although he fit in as just another one of the boys, we held him in high esteem.

Nicholas Poccia

*The Eastman Symphony Band in the Eastman Theater, circa early 1950s.
Photo by Louis Ouzer.*

John Beck

I first met Dr. Fennell in 1951 as a freshman percussionist in the Eastman Symphonic Band. During my four years at Eastman, I performed in all the groups he conducted. I was in the first Wind Ensemble and the first recordings of that group. After leaving Eastman for four years and returning in 1959 as a member of the Rochester Philharmonic Orchestra and faculty member of Eastman, my association with Fred became that of a colleague. I watched him mold the Eastman Wind Ensemble into a major musical force and administer the Ensemble Department of Eastman with equal skill.

Fred is dynamic. Both on and off the podium, he is a person of which people are aware. There is not a single member of his wind ensemble that does not have respect for him. He inspires a group to perform much better than they thought was possible. Some of my most memorable moments as a student come from rehearsals and performances with Fred on the podium. He was firm but never mean. A saying of his that inspires me is, "you can produce good music by fear or by kindness; I prefer kindness."

Fred represents the Wind Ensemble in American music. There are few musicians who don't know Fred Fennell. His personality is infectious. Whether conducting or speaking, he commands attention. Now, in the coda of his life and career, he still possesses an enormous amount of energy and drive.

John Beck
Professor of Percussion
Eastman School of Music

Sam Fricano

When I reported to the Eastman School of Music in September 1951, I was a young trumpet player focused on becoming a well-trained symphony trumpeter. There wasn't a school orchestra in my small high school in Silver Creek, New York, but I had played in several all-state orchestras and an excellent community symphony in the Buffalo area. I enjoyed playing in wind bands, but didn't have the same fervor for that medium that I had for orchestral playing. Frederick Fennell called a meeting of about 40 wind, brass and percussion players in May 1952, and explained to us his concept of a Wind Ensemble he would begin organizing and rehearsing in September of that year. This was a novel approach for that time, in that most of the doubling on parts that was standard in larger symphonic or concert bands would be eliminated. There would be much more responsibility on each individual's shoulders than there would be in a typical concert band of that era. It sounded like a great idea to us, and we couldn't wait to get started in September.

The combination of Fred's enthusiasm, musical insight and conducting skills, teamed with this new instrumentation, made an instant impact on all of us. The Eastman Wind Ensemble soon became an exceptional musical organization, and Fred Fennell's imagination and programming skills exposed us to the best available wind band music. Distinguished composers soon felt compelled to write new compositions for band and wind ensemble, and within a few years there was a whole new generation of outstanding musicians who composed specifically for the wind ensemble. Those of us who were fortunate to be a part of the original Eastman Wind Ensemble realized quite early that this was something

*The first Eastman Wind Ensemble, 1952.
Photo courtesy of the Eastman School of Music, Louis Ouzer, photographer.*

very special – but I don't think any of us, including Fred, realized that we were a part of a new chapter in music history. As the years have passed, my appreciation has only grown for what was accomplished by Fred Fennell's Wind Ensembles, and I think all of us who played in that organization have experienced a lifetime of pride as a result of being so intimately involved in the beginning of a new era in music for winds. For this young trumpeter from Silver Creek, New York, Dr. Fennell forever changed my appreciation of what can be accomplished every time I have seen him over the years, and I am still amazed at the vitality and skill he possesses after a career of more than seven decades.

Sam Fricano

FF, Aaron Copland and Serge Koussevitsky (1874-1951) at the Berkshire Music Center in 1948. © 1987 The Instrumentalist Co. Reprinted with permission.

Norman Schweikert

I have so many fond memories of making music and socializing with Fred over the past 45 years it is hard to know where to begin. We first met in Rochester in 1955 when, as a teenager, I came from Los Angeles to join the Rochester Civic Philharmonic, and Eastman-Rochester Symphony Orchestras. I soon enrolled in the Eastman School of Music to pursue an undergraduate degree and found myself in the enviable position of being both a professional player in a major U.S. orchestra and a student at one of America's finest music schools.

As a student, I was obliged to participate in the school's performing organizations. In 1957, I became a member of the Eastman Wind Ensemble, serving as assistant first horn to my dear friend Aubrey Bouck. Aubrey graduated the following year, and I became the ensemble's principal horn and spent the next three years in that position under Fred's inspiring leadership. In my four years with this wonderful organization, Fred introduced me to the magnificent wind ensemble repertoire, a gift that he bestowed with energy, enthusiasm, and dedication. His knowledge of wind music is expansive, and we all were the beneficiaries of it.

I vividly remember the 1:00 p.m. rehearsals on the second floor of the Eastman Theater Annex. As a short warm-up, Fred started such rehearsals with the last eight bars of *Ein Heldenleben*. I believe he was influenced by the 1954 Reiner recording of this Strauss work with the Chicago Symphony Orchestra because he would often make reference to its brass. I recall him saying to us, "Brass, I want that chord to sound like a solid block of concrete – just like the Chicago Symphony's brass section." Little did I dream that I would later become part of that Chicago sound.

The Eastman Wind Ensemble, which Fred founded in 1952, was the elite performing organization at Eastman and included the best wind players the school had to offer. It was inevitable that such a fine ensemble would be recorded for posterity, and this was indeed realized. Mercury Records took up the task and produced a number of excellent recordings. I was fortunate to have performed on more than a dozen discs. Sousa marches were part of Fred's favorite repertoire, and we recorded two albums of them—no one did them better! For the recordings he had baffles put behind the horn section and requested us to play the after-beats with bells up for maximum rhythmic vitality. When test pressings were received, Fred would have ensemble members over to his house to hear the results on his newly acquired Pro-Plane speakers. These were state of the art at that time and came as a gift from the company in recognition of his high quality recordings. I recall that he played for us the just-released recording of *Das Rheingold* with Solti and the Vienna Philharmonic—quite a delight through those speakers. Two albums made to document original band music of the American Civil War have special meaning to me. For this, Fred, after much research, found authentic hand-written band books for both the North (Port Royal Band, 3rd New Hampshire Regiment) and the South (26th North Carolina Regiment Band). The small brass band of the rebel organization was missing its bass (tuba) part. Fred spread out all the other part books and reconstructed the bass part for each tune. The result certainly sounds convincingly accurate!

Upon leaving the wind ensemble, graduates were presented with a special award, which was inscribed as follows: THE EASTMAN SYMPHONIC WIND ENSEMBLE, Frederick Fennell, Conductor, and its EXCLUSIVE and Honorable Society of Ching ffOOM HEREBY RECOGNIZES THE UNIQUE PERSONAGE: [name inserted here] and extends the thanks of all its distinguished membership to the same in recognition of: [details of membership, titles, of albums recorded, special TV shows and trips, all in Fred's hand], Dated _{inserted}_ Rochester, New York [signed ff]. The title of this award came from the signature crash of the cymbals (Ching) followed by the resounding stroke on the bass drum (ffOOM) on consecutive after beats in the closing bars of a Sousa march. He gave this name to one of his sailboats, and I believe there was a Ching Foom II as well!

Drawing by FF.

Beginning in 1954 and continuing for several years, Fred conducted the Eastman Chamber Orchestra in five weekly concerts plus a symposium of student works. I was most fortunate to play second horn in this group for four summers: 1957-60. Fred's selection of repertoire followed this plan, as stated on the back of the program for the final concert of the 1958 season: "In the five seasons past, we have uncovered but a few of the rich musical treasures that lie about in such abundance. We have followed a

David Hall, Bob Fine and FF just before the first recording session of the EWE. This was Bob Fine's recording truck. Photo courtesy of FF, May, 1953.

FF with composer Leroy Anderson during a Mercury recording, 1953. Photo courtesy of William L. Decker.

consistent policy of not repeating repertoire, preferring instead to present a continual unfolding of attractive materials from all periods of orchestral development." Needless to say, I was introduced to a wide variety of eclectic repertoire, playing many pieces for the first time (including Bach's wonderful *Brandenburg Concerto No. 1* with my colleague and teacher, Morris Secon). Fred told me that after the final concert of a season, he would spread out his materials on the floor at home and immediately plan the next season's concerts.

With the Eastman-Rochester Pops Orchestra, Fred recorded a few albums of light music. These included works of Leroy Anderson and Percy Grainger, all performed with the usual Fennell energy and devotion to the integrity of the compositions. I can still picture Fred playing the typewriter himself on the podium for Anderson's popular tune by that name.

When I left Rochester for a faculty position at the Interlochen Arts Academy in 1966, my wife, Sally, son, Eric, and I could expect to see Fred and his wife during the summers at their cabin in "The Orchestra Colony" on the shores of Duck Lake. It was a social occasion, which we eagerly anticipated, partly for its annual barbecue. Fred would stack up the charcoal in a wire basket suspended above the grill, soak the briquettes with lighter fluid, and strike a match. We would then sing *The Stars and Stripes Forever* a couple of times, with all repeats, and then the charcoal was deemed ready for the grill. The hot coals would be released from the basket and Fred would begin the barbecuing. Over dinner, we would talk about our various activities from the past year, soak up history from Fred's tales of his many earlier adventures, and indulge in remembrances of our wind ensemble days together. It was always a happy time. A few years later, when I joined the Chicago Symphony Orchestra, Fred would often call when he was in town for the Midwest Band Clinic and we'd catch up on things. It was also fortunate that we were able to meet with him in Tokyo during one of the Chicago Symphony tours and enjoy a fine meal together. I still can hear him answering the telephone with "moshi-moshi," as is the custom in that country.

Memories of Fred extend into the next generation as well. Our son, Eric, timpanist of the Fort Wayne Philharmonic since 1989, had, as a young student, an impromptu percussion lesson during one of Fred's visits to our home. Later on, as a member of the World Youth Symphony Orchestra at Interlochen, Eric performed in the percussion section under Fred's direction. Eric remembers that "Uncle Fred" would always bring his special bass drum beaters for the section to use when he was conducting. One was a large, heavy, wooden beater covered with chamois. Eventually, as the beater traveled around, the chamois would wear out and Fred would have to recover the mallet. Eric is the proud owner of one of these worn-out pieces, which Fred autographed for him. Eric also recollects the volume required for the bass drum notes. Fred would go over the note heads with a magic marker, making the heads of soft notes small and loud ones large (some almost the size of a penny). There was no need to look at dynamics when playing one of Fred's bass drum parts, and when he wanted it loud, it had to reflect his signature: FF!

The years have been kind to us, and we are all grateful to have had Fred as an inspiration as well as a true friend.

Norman Schweikert,
Chicago Symphony Orchestra (retired)

Doris Preucil

Fred Fennell is an inspired conductor and "orchestra trainer." His insistence on clarity, releases, and listening developed awareness and self-discipline, while his love of music evoked our best efforts. His choice of repertoire, both in Junior Orchestra and in Little Symphony, opened new musical worlds for us.

It was a wonderful opportunity for me to be a concertmaster in Fennell's orchestras. I came to Eastman with professional orchestra experience but lacked confidence as a soloist. At the first rehearsal of *Til Eulenspiegel*, the violin solo was easy until I reached the top E-flat before the long descending glissando. I felt suspended on a high precipice and held onto that note for dear life. The friendly hazing that followed is one of my more amusing memories.

In 1998, my student orchestra met one of my "musical heroes" when Fred Fennell was its guest conductor at the Midwest International Band and Orchestra Conference. The photo from that event hangs in our school waiting room to this day.

Doris Preucil
Preucil School of Music

EWE, 1953.
Photo by Louis Ouser.

Tom Miller

During the first year or so following the creation of the EWE, there was a series of open rehearsals transmitted throughout New York State. This broadcast was performed in cooperation with the New York State School of Music Association. Fred would stop the group at various points to stress certain elements and to make corrections. At the end of the rehearsal, there was a nonstop play-through incorporating, presumably, the improvements. During the rehearsal, Fred would call out to various players or sections, for instance, "a little more forceful there trombones" or "very nice Patrica."

During breaks in the action, Fred would say something like "the euphonium solo in that passage was played by Tom Miller from Syracuse, New York" or "the lovely trumpet playing you heard was by Bill Lockwood, who comes from Elmira, New York." The only people mentioned by name were those whose hometowns were in-state; out of state players—the majority—were shut out! This led to the informal creation of a tongue-in-cheek society within the EWE made up of those identified by name and hometown on one of the NYSSMA broadcasts.

No doubt, Fred had his reasons for this. Listeners throughout the state would find it intriguing that students from familiar towns played such excellent music. Thus, these broadcasts served a recruiting purpose in that talented high-school students would be encouraged to apply to Eastman.

Tom Miller

Kenley Inglefield

Frederick Fennell changed the course of my life, although I'm not sure that he didn't have that in mind when he called me to his office at the Eastman School of Music in the fall of 1953. I had auditioned at Eastman on both cello and trombone and was accepted as a music education major on either instrument. Naturally, I did the sensible thing and chose cello as my instrument; then, as now, string teachers were in demand.

Early in my freshman year, Dr. Fennell heard that I doubled on euphonium in high school. He needed euphonium players for the Symphonic Band, and I got a note summoning me to his office. In return for playing euphonium in the band, he would arrange a scholarship to cover euphonium lessons in addition to cello lessons.

As a result, I studied euphonium for a year with Donald Knaub, a fine teacher and great gentleman. Following that, I studied for three years with the legendary "chief," Emory Remington. Two years in the Symphonic Band were followed by two years in the Eastman Wind Ensemble. Still being sensible, I continued to study cello.

After graduation, I avoided the draft by playing in The U.S. Army Band in Washington, D.C. Over the years, opportunities to play trombone and euphonium have continued; I haven't played cello in thirty years, and I owe it all to that note from Frederick Fennell.

Kenley Inglefield
Director, Elkhart County Youth Orchestra

Eastman Wind Ensemble, 1954.
Photo by Louis Ouzer, courtesy of the Eastman School.

FF and the EWE in the Eastman Theater, 1954-55 (the 3rd EWE).
Photo by Louis Ouzer.

On the podium at Eastman in 1956.
Photo by Louis Ouzer.

Photo by Louis Ouzer.

Gretel Y. Shanly

My introduction to Frederick Fennell came when I was a member of the Eastman Junior Orchestra and he was the conductor. He programmed truly professional, standard repertoire, including *Capriccio Espanole* and works by Debussy and Rossini. The program was challenging and was truly a great help to me later in my career. The thrill of playing *Scheherazade* in the flute solos at the tender age of eighteen. Looking back now, I appreciate his clear-cut beat, well-prepared interpretations and straightforward way of dealing with performers.

Later, I was assigned to the first Eastman Wind Ensemble. One day, the piccolo player was absent so I unthinkingly filled in. At the next rehearsal, I was shocked to discover that I was now scheduled to perform the piccolo on the first recording; this recording included the treacherous unaccompanied long solo E in the Persechetti. I resumed as first flute for the next recordings.

While working in the movie industry and in making solo recordings and ensemble discs, including a number with the Westwood Wind Quintet, this recording experience came in handy for me. In the Eastman Wind Ensemble, I particularly appreciated his decision to seat flutes facing the audience rather than facing them towards the back of the stage as so many bands do today.

Here on Kaua'i this summer, I hosted four flutists from the girls' Tachibana Senior High School near Kyoto. Despite the language barrier, we discovered that the founder of the spectacular marching and concert band was, of course, familiar with Fennell's work and appreciated my connection with Eastman.

I give thanks for being a part of the fine tradition that Fennell created.

Gretel Y. Shanly, flutist

On the podium at Eastman in 1956. Photo by Louis Ouzer.

Richard Hoffman

It was 1953 or 1954 and Dr. Fennell was conducting a dress rehearsal of an undergraduate symphonic concert on the stage of the Eastman Theater. When it came time to do the Brahms double concerto, Ray Gniewek and Ira Lehn strode out from the wings, took their places, tuned their instruments lightly to the oboe's "A," and indicated that they were ready to start. Dr. Fennell turned to the orchestra and lifted his baton. Suddenly he froze in mid-preparation, turned his head, and did a classic double take as he realized that Ira was holding Ray's violin and Ray had Ira's cello between his legs.

Richard Hoffman
ESM 1955

EWE 1956.
Photo courtesy of Louis Ouzer.

Photo by Louis Ouzer.

Photo by Louis Ouzer.

In Kilbourn Hall at the Eastman School. Photo courtesy of Eastman School of Music.

Tanya Lesinsky Carey

Fred Fennell has been a part of my life since my high school days. He judged a high school contest in which I played; he wrote "bravo" on the sheet and gave me all ones. I still have the sheet. The next year I was at Eastman and played in his orchestra.

Fred asked me to join his run-out orchestra in Batavia. It was most memorable squeezing the cello, Fred, and I in his new sports car on those hour-long drives. My husband and I had our first child after my first summer in graduate school at Eastman. Fred was always a supportive mentor and friend. I remember breaking down in his office when I realized I could not juggle two school orchestras, a baby, recitals, and library hours for research on my musicology degree. He calmed me down and said, "I'll see what can be done." Within the week, Howard Hanson, the famed director of Eastman, called me into his office to explain the new performance master's degree. I would be one of the first in the program, and all of my credits would be retroactive. I am forever grateful to Fred for the music, the mentoring, the fun, and the friendship.

Tanya Lesinsky Carey

Photo by Louis Ouzer.

Harold Lawrence, FF and Wilma Cozart Fine of Mercury Recordings reviewing editions for recording. Photo courtesy of Louis Ouzer, circa 1956.

Photo of Frederick Fennell sent to Betty Ludwig in 1986 from a 1956 photo. Courtesy of Elizabeth Ludwig Fennell.

Gordon Peters

My time with Fred encompassed six years at Eastman: 1953-59. I came to Eastman as a sophomore after serving three years in the West Point Band. I played in the Wind Ensemble for five years and performed many times under Fred with the band, orchestra, and Rochester Philharmonic.

It was with the Wind Ensemble that I learned the most from him. His energy, talents, and dedication to the Wind Ensemble concept were extraordinary. I clearly recall Fennell's ear and care for articulation and nuance. (On a side note, Fennell routinely shouted "SHORT!" at the players because they were not playing a truly clear staccato.) Watching him edit the music, particularly those works to be recorded by Mercury Records, was a lesson in itself. Hearing and watching Fred respond constructively sharpened our ears. Above all, he was a good friend and a true educator. Here are a few anecdotes relating Fennell's influence on my career.

During my years at Eastman, I formed a marimba ensemble: The Marimba Masters. We were fortunate in getting many engagements, and on one occasion, we had booked a concert months ahead of time. Unwittingly, Fred scheduled a wind ensemble concert on the same date. He graciously let us keep the date and used the young percussion students in school for his concert.

Photo by Louis Ouzer, circa late 1950s. Courtesy of the Eastman School.

I vividly recall the role Fennell played in the genesis of master's thesis for the McHose Theory Department. When I began my thesis, McHose, of course, wanted me to write on a theory subject, something like counting lute tablatures. However, I wanted to write on percussion, for I did not want to leave Eastman without knowing something about the history of the instrument family with which I was involved. We also started the percussion/marimba ensemble program at Eastman at this time, in addition to some auxiliary projects that needed to be codified. Fred consented to meet with McHose to "bend" McHose's ear; the meeting lasted 45 minutes, and McHose finally consented. The work was called *"Treatise of Percussion,"* which entailed 417 pages and two and a half years of work. Later, I hired a professional editor and published the work. Nineteen of the original 3,500 copies remain. At the time, there were rumblings of an emerging national percussion organization, and retrospectively, this opus was one of the cornerstones of this movement. Without Fred, this work may never have come to fruition.

Gordon Peters

Stephen Seiffert

I first met Dr. Fennell in the fall of 1956 when I entered the Eastman School of Music as a French horn and music history major. I not only knew Dr. Fennell as the conductor of the famed Eastman Wind Ensemble, of which I was a member from 1957 through 1960, but also as my advisor who helped me through many rough spots. He often talked about himself, his experiences at Interlochen in the early years, and what he wanted to accomplish before he was fifty. I remember one story he told about the time at Interlochen when he dropped a cymbal during a rehearsal at the Interlochen Bowl; it cascaded down the risers crashing as it hit each lower level.

It was an exciting time to be at Eastman and especially to be a member of the Wind Ensemble. Fennell, as students referred to him, was very active in Music Education circles and often spoke at conventions. In one of those speeches, he emphasized the importance of music educators' involvement in community activities, especially in small towns. Someone from Batavia, New York was looking for a conductor for their community orchestra. This individual came to him after the talk and suggested that he lead by example and take over the conductorship of their orchestra. At that point, he couldn't say no and took on the task in addition to his duties at the Eastman School.

At the first rehearsal, he was dismayed to find that the orchestra lacked some critical players. As a result, he solicited several of us, who were at that time second year students at Eastman, to join the Batavia Symphony. Sandra Flesher, Robert Sheldon, Tania Lasinsky, and I traveled weekly to Batavia with Fennell to rehearse with the orchestra. When the weather was bad, we took the train, which was a milk run from Buffalo to Albany. On one occasion, the passenger car was quite full, and we were forced to stand. Fennell noticed that the conductor had taken over four seats for himself and showed no intention of relinquishing any of them. Fennell approached the man and berated him, at which point the man capitulated and turned over two of the seats so the girls could sit. I have never forgotten this incident because it showed a side of Fennell of which few others knew. He could not stand to be treated with anything less than the respect he thought he deserved.

It was an exciting time to be a member of the Wind Ensemble. It was a crackerjack group, which made something like ten recordings during that time.

A great many of these players joined orchestras in cities like Chicago, New York, Cleveland, Los Angeles, Detroit, Baltimore, Buffalo, and Toronto. The wind ensemble rehearsals were packed with excitement, enthusiasm, and, above all, discipline. There was no messing around with Fennell, who never minced words. He worked very efficiently, which contributed greatly to the quality of the group. The group also benefited from his emphasis on accurate and strict rhythm.

I recall the time we were preparing the *High School Cadets* march. He wanted to emphasize the first three beats of the main melody and instructed all of the percussionists to strike on these beats. This included a bass drummer, timpanist, and six snare drummers all double sticking those beats. The sound was so overwhelming

Conducting a recording session with the Eastman — Rochester Orchestra probably in 1958-59. Photo courtesy of Louis Ouzer.

These photos show the placement of double pear-shaped Telefunken microphones and the monaural LP pickup mikes. Several other Telefunkens made the recordings cutting edge stereophonic. Courtesy of Eastman School of Music, Paul White and Louis Ouzer.

Eastman Wind Ensemble rehearsal, 1950s. Photo was a gift to the Sibley Library by Paul White. Photo courtesy of Eastman School of Music.

that the rest of the players could not be heard over the percussion. After several rehearsals, some of the players decided to play a little trick on Fennell. Eventually, every non-percussionist agreed that when we rehearsed *High School Cadets* they would not play at all for those three beats. Fennell enjoyed the sound of the percussion so much that he never knew the difference. I often of think these experiences and long to return to these efficient, energy packed rehearsals, especially when playing in an orchestra with a long-winded conductor.

Chief Kei-He-San-Ah Ate Tau-Atoa
(which means: Chief Little Man with Big Stick).

I have crossed paths with Dr. Fennell a number of times since 1960. I believe the last time was in 1977 when we both visited Interlochen. Later, he guest conducted a concert of contemporary American music while I was principal French horn in Buffalo. He was conducting a work by Leon Kirchner, and the first rehearsal did not go well; it looked like he couldn't handle the mixed meters. As it turned out, the score he had been sent did not agree with the parts, and when he realized this he flew into a rage, threw the score onto the podium, and stomped on it. This was another example in which he had not been treated with the proper respect. When an accurate score was finally produced, his demeanor completely changed, and everything came off without a hitch.

I don't know if this is public knowledge, but in the late 50s, he was made an honorary Indian Chief and was given an Indian name that means "Little Man With a Big Stick." I owe a great deal to Frederick Fennell, not only for the wonderful training I got playing under his baton, but also for instilling in me a continuing love and curiosity. One of the first contacts I had with the man was at Eastman in 1956. Fennell spoke at a Phi Mu Alpha smoker about Rimsky-Korsakov's *Scheherazade*. I just played the work in a high school youth orchestra, and so I knew it well. Somehow, Fennell's talk brought the music to life; every time I perform the work, I think of him.

Stephen Seiffert,
BM, DMA Eastman, MA Brown,
MSC Queens University

```
WESTERN UNION
TELEGRAM

cBYA069 PA257

P ATA051 PD=ATLANTIC CITY NJER 20 210PME=
=PERCY ALDRIDGE GRAINGER, DONT PHONE=
    7 CROMWELL PL WHITE PLAINS NY=

=FATES MOST UNKIND IN PREVENTING YOUR BEING WITH US
TONIGHT BUT AS ALWAYS YOU ARE THE POSY IN OUR BUTTON
HOLE, AFFECTIONATELY=
    FREDERICK FENNELL AND EASTMAN WIND ENSEMBLE.
```

FF and composer Alec Wilder, 1959. Photo courtesy of the Eastman School.

Rehearsal at Eastman, notice the "LISTEN" banner. Alec Wilder is listening. Photo courtesy of the Eastman School.

David Fetter

While I was a student at the Eastman School from 1955-60, FF conducted the Eastman Wind Ensemble, but also, sometimes to his frustration, Orchestra II and the rather large Symphonic Band. The latter was the opposite of the lean precise Wind Ensemble.

Fennell characteristically shouted, "wait!" before, say, an eighth note pickup and a downbeat. While he may have developed this to combat the tendency of young people to rush, the effect of waiting but still trying to play in time could add a dramatic effect.

At that time, the large ensemble always played after Fennell's beat. This was a constant topic of study and debate among the students, which we never resolved.

David Fetter
Associate Dean for Performance Activities
and Placement Conservatory
and Preparatory Trombone Faculties
Peabody Institute

Barry Benjamin

In my freshman year at the Eastman School, I played first horn in the junior orchestra. I was an eighteen-year-old kid from Brooklyn with no high register. Fred selected the Schumann *Rhennish Symphony* for the program that year. I was in big trouble! One, but only one, of the problems was the horn and trombone unison at the start of the slow movement. It goes on and on, up and up, culminating in a sustained E-flat—B-flat above the staff for horn. I was as good as dead. The trombone player was another freshman, Porter Poindexter. He did everything well.

I never hit the B-flat in the rehearsals. At the performance, we began the slow movement, and I was playing very well. We began to go up, and I had hope. All the notes were coming out. I went for the high B-flat, and nothing came out—no sound at all. Behind me, Porter poured out the most gorgeous B-flat. While I didn't get a sound, I did get red, and it was clear I was blowing. Fred looked at us and smiled. What a unison! It truly sounded like one player. On the next note, I managed to fall back in and we finished the concert. To this day, I'm not sure that Fred knows I never hit the high note.

During my time at Eastman, I grew tremendously as a musician and later took a job as Professor of Horn at the University of Wisconsin-Milwaukee. One morning in the late 1980s, the phone rang and a voice on the other end asked me if I recognized the music coming over the line. I recognized it as an obscure piece of wind music by Florent Schmidt titled *Lied and Scherzo*. The voice then asked if I knew the horn soloist, and I thought that it was, in fact, me. "Right again," replied the voice, "now do you know who this is?" It had to be Frederick Fennell. After all these years, he remembered me and asked me to play the piece with him at the Library of Congress. What a memory the man possesses.

I have numerous other memories of Fred, but perhaps the greatest is that Fred always treated the musicians under him very well. I have a great deal of respect and affection for him.

Barry Benjamin
University of Wisconsin

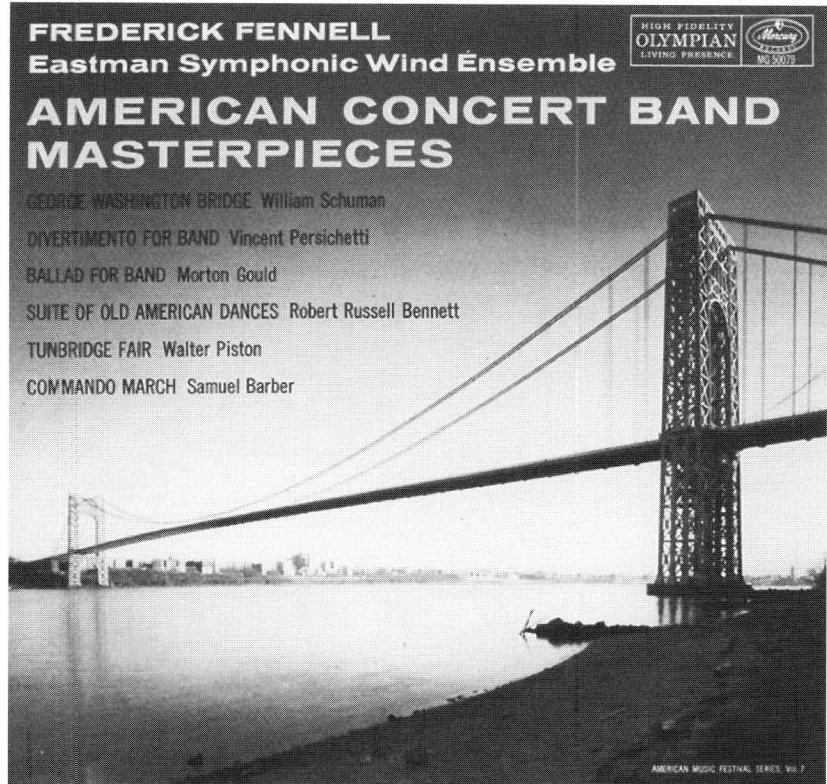

Photo of album by Louis Ouzer courtesy of the Eastman School and Universal Polygram.

Roger Sherman

I am extremely happy to have had the opportunity to work with Dr. Frederick Fennell in the late 1950s, when I was a member of the Eastman Wind Ensemble. Performing with him and the group radically shaped my musical future and has contributed more than I can ever articulate to my success in the music profession.

I have been fortunate to perform with most of the world's major orchestral conductors during the latter half of the Twentieth Century. From my work with these artists, I recall the precision with which the Eastman Wind Ensemble played under Dr. Fennell's direction. I often felt that most of these conductors could not elicit the same degree of precision. I still remember with a smile the rare occasions when Dr. Fennell would become impatient with the work of the brass section. He would say, with some degree of exasperation, "I hope you didn't come here just to blow spit on the floor."

Roger Sherman
Trumpeter, Pittsburgh Symphony Orchestra

As tall as Howard Hanson was, he fit right in FF's 1954 TF MG arriving at the Fennell Shed - Interlochen, 1959. Photo courtesy of FF.

The Fennell summer cottage "Driftwoods" at Interlochen, MI.

Ronald Bishop

I first met Dr. Frederick Fennell at Tally-Ho Music Camp near Rochester, N.Y. Over my six years at this camp, I performed concerts, played softball and tennis, and, in my final year, actually put on a roof with "Dr. Fred." FF manned the extremely dull Skil saw, and I handled the flashlight as we worked past dark.

Like most camps, Tally-Ho had "skit night," and I remember that parents enjoyed my "monkey on a string" imitation of my respected conductor. In the summer of 2001, I played under FF with the Blossom Festival Band, and he reminded me of another skit I did of a slow motion baseball game. The skit took place in 1949, and he remembered it in detail—truly remarkable.

Taken from the back of Ronald Bishop in rehearsal at Severance Hall 2004. Courtesy of the Cleveland Orchestra. Photo by Roger Mastroianni.

During my years at the Eastman School of Music (1952-56), the Cleveland Orchestra, and the Cleveland Symphonic Winds it was, and very much still is, my privilege to work with The Maestro. I perpetually use two of his phrases in my own teaching: "finger fortissimo" and "play it ten times shorter than you think you can and it still won't be short enough."

I am thrilled and honored to add my thanks and appreciation to the untold number of us who benefited from knowing, working with, and learning from the inspiring human being we know as "Freddie" Fennell.

Ronald Bishop
Principal Tuba Cleveland Orchestra

FF at his first American Band Masters Association with Karl King and Henry Fillmore, 1958. Photo courtesy of FF.

Frederick receiving a hood for his Honary Doctorate at Oklahoma City University. Left is Clustor Smith, FF, Bishop Angie Smith and Clarence Burg, 1959. Photo courtesy of the Eastman School.

*Eastman Philharmonia Tour - Buffalo Festival, 1959.
Photo courtesy of the Eastman School.*

Robert E. Sheldon

Like many Fennell fans, I first became acquainted with his work via the early Mercury recordings of the Eastman Wind Ensemble. They spun on my cheap turntable for hours at a time. One of my high-school friends had been to the National Music Camp at Interlochen during the summer of 1954, and he inspired me to join him there the following summer. Fennell, of course, was a fixture at Interlochen, and I first met him there. In addition to his great conducting routine, he often scouted promising students for Eastman at the camp. I was so honored. Thanks to Frederick Fennell, my Eastman class of 1960, in addition to those of 1959 and 1961, included some real future superstars such as Roger Bobo, Larry Combs, Peter Hadcock, James Austin, and Robert Gillespie.

Since having the pleasure of playing in his ensembles, I have enjoyed occasional and all too rare Fennell performances. The most recent of these performances was May 19, 2001 in the Coolidge Auditorium of the Library of Congress. The concert featured a thirty-six piece wind band playing American music. The Maestro even performed some rudimental field drumming on a nineteenth-century rope-tension instrument. He joined the three piccolo players to offer examples of eighteenth- and nineteenth-century fife and drum music: a rare treat for all in attendance.

Fennell band concerts generally close with three marches performed in his very special way. For those marches played on this program, our thirty-six piece band instantly grew to forty-one as five old Eastmanites came on stage to surprise him with a guest appearance. No rehearsal was necessary; Fennell fans know how he does Sousa. It became a sort of mini-reunion with a concert attached, and the good vibes and electricity on stage and in the auditorium were apparent to everyone present.

Fennell has conducted concerts on our series several times, including works by such composers as Strauss, Mozart, and Hindemith. For all of these and a lot more, Fennell might or might not have a score on his stand. He seems to be rather like Dimitri Mitropoulos, who preferred to do his work from memory so he could enjoy watching the musicians.

Fred is a dynamic, yet endearingly humble leader. He is just another one of the musicians, so to speak. If the ensemble includes sixty members, he is simply the sixty-first and happens to play his part from the podium. A Fennell rehearsal is not only a rehearsal but also an informal staff meeting full of good humor. Every ensemble, whether it's a high-school group from a remote area of the country or a top-drawer London orchestra, receives one hundred percent of his positive treatment and attention. The man simply makes one feel good about the process, one's part in it, and the art itself.

We all know him, of course, in the field of wind band and wind ensemble music, but not enough people know him as a world-class orchestral conductor. The Minneapolis Orchestra certainly thought of him as such when they wisely engaged him as Associate Conductor following his resignation from the Eastman School faculty. A few members of the Orchestra, during Fennell's time there, have indicated to me the pure artistic delight of just playing anything, including "kiddie concerts," with their Associate Conductor. He shared music-making with them, showing the delight it can, and should, provide.

Most of my cherished Fennell memories involve orchestral episodes. There were, of course, the Eastman School orchestras under his direction, but the town of Batavia, New York also engaged him to lead their civic orchestra. Batavians populated the orchestra as much as possible, but Fennell would bring in Eastman students to fill the holes as necessary. Those were wonderful moments watching him mold and teach an earnest, amateur ensemble of diverse talents. I am certain that the housewife on violin who worried about her technical problems on the fingerboard left those rehearsals feeling good about nearly everything.

Once I rode over to Batavia in his MG convertible, the top of which was definitely not designed for comfort in upper New York winters. He loved that car. As soon as we got into some good shop talk, the weather conditions faded from notice. I've occasionally wondered if that MG accompanied him to his Florida residence where the climate better suited the car. A library colleague recently assured me that it is, indeed, there.

A Fennell orchestral performance took place at the Eastman School, which has, for a number of years, produced what they call Prism Concerts. They involve clever lighting effects and the in-theater hydraulic lifting machinery so that one ensemble immediately follows another. I attended one of those events at which Dr. Fennell received an honorary degree. He turned to face the Eastman Philharmonic, which magically emerged from the shadows and mounted the podium with his wonderful mix of flair and humility. That evening, he conducted the Respighi *Fountains of Rome*. Of course, he didn't use a score. It was all stored away forever in his mind, and I have to assume that his band schedules were such that he had not performed the piece with an orchestra in years.

Fennell's interests are manifold and delve into the historical aspects of music. As an Eastman student attempting to start an antique woodwind and brass collection, I occasionally took my latest find to his office for a show-and-tell session.

Unusual set up for performance and recording of music of the Civil War. All are facing different directions–even FF is in the top back facing the audience. Heterodox arrangement of FF. Photo courtesy of Polygram Universal.

His historical inclinations strongly focus on early band music and related military lore. Many of us know about his youthful years in the Cleveland area where his family maintained a sort of pseudo-military encampment called "Camp Zeke." Camp Zeke activities included a lot of rudimental field drumming, which he still does with great style; he displayed his finesse on the field drum during our May 19 Library concert. His musical military interest culminated at Eastman with the realization of his desire to record brass band music and other music of the Civil War era on as much period equipment as possible.

Procuring said equipment was not a problem. In those days, Fennell was already on the road as a conductor-in-demand and therefore was no stranger to the airlines. He made all the necessary arrangements and dragged me aboard a plane headed for the District of Columbia. My duties at the Smithsonian included selecting a set of band instruments, preferably over-the-left-shoulder models.

They were the most popular and efficient models and were typical of the militia bands of the mid-nineteenth century.

Fennell then pursued his quest at the Library of Congress which was reputed to have a surviving set of manuscripts from one of the larger militia bands from New Hampshire. It was true, and their challenging contents indicated that the old band was likely one of the better ones of the period. Comparable sets of surviving music were preserved at the Moravian Music Foundation in Old Salem, North Carolina. The recording project of his dreams was well underway.

The first rehearsal was quite a mind-blower—definitely not the norm for students at a conservatory. Discovering each new piece seemed like real pioneering without driving prairie schooners. It was especially wonderful to watch Fennell react to each quaint harmonic or melodic gem that surfaced from those nineteenth-century pages. The Eastman Wind Ensemble, with its array of backwards pointing horns, played all of this nineteenth-century literature in an Eastman Theatre performance. We were on our normal risers, but we faced backwards with the horns pointing toward the audience. Fennell, also facing the audience, was perched highest of all on the back of the stage. It was enjoyable to share his humorous observations about conducting "downhill." He discusses all of this in the extensive performance notes for his two civil war albums.

Hearing *Our Musical Past* still brings back a flood of good memories. It was for a similar nineteenth-century band project in which Fennell acted as both conductor and bass drummer. However, his double duty worked for a rehearsal or two. Having Fennell's expressive hands impeded with a drumbeater was clearly a waste, and so we happily engaged a bass drummer and returned the Maestro to the podium. *(See photo page 110)*

Outside the Pavillion at Wolf Trap standing on a red, white and blue bass drum podium of Bill Ludwig's. Beside FF is Robert (Bob) E. Sheldon, 1974. Courtesy Bob Sheldon

The summer of 1974 was also enjoyable thanks to Dr. Fennell. He had been asked to do a concert at Wolf Trap, one featuring marches from his famous albums. The Concert included, not only Sousa and Fillmore, but also concert marches such as *Crown Imperial* by Sir William Walton and *Broadway Fare* by Gershwin and Rodgers. He asked me to contract a fairly large concert band, and I got to play my old Eastman Wind Ensemble spot: third horn and first E-flat tenorhorn. Notably, the podium was a red, white, and blue bass drum, suitably revised for the Maestro by Bill Ludwig.

While I have numerous other memories of the Maestro, let me conclude with a playful image of the great man and his favorite local brew: Genesee 12-Horse. His preferred vessel for enjoying said product solved the problem of frequent refills. It was, I think, a small glass goldfish bowl, which looked rather like a giant brandy snifter. Let us always continue to celebrate this singular musician and human being.

Robert E. Sheldon
Music Division, Library of Congress

Jim Badolato

My memories of Frederick Fennell go back to the Eastman Wind Ensemble, in which I played for three years. His ideas and interpretations have made an indelible impression on some of the ways that I approach playing. However, I would not have attended Eastman if not for Dr. Fennell. I was turned down as a composition major, but Dr. Fennell heard my clarinet tape and suggested that I apply as a clarinet major. I got into the school and thereby received a great foundation for a wonderful career as a clarinetist and college professor.

Because he took the time to direct my application process to Eastman and because of my contact with him at the Eastman Wind Ensemble, I will never forget Dr. Fennell. In fact, I still carry a note that he sent me on the night of my Performer's performance at Eastman in my clarinet case.

Jim Badolato
ESM 1960

Demonstrating a 19th-century over-the-shoulder large bore E-flat bass. Photo courtesy of Universal Polygram, 1960.

Jay Berliner

I have fond memories of Frederick Fennell, memories going way back to 1960 when I was fortunate enough to play under him in the Eastman School Symphony Orchestra. The program for that session included Brahms's *Second Symphony*. I remember Dr. Fennell discussing with great passion and exacting detail how Brahms wrote across the bar line, which was revolutionary in his day. It was challenging for Fennell to convey to his students the subtleties of this free approach to classical composition.

After a series of agonizing, yet invigorating rehearsals, the musicians finally understood the concept. The performance by the lowest-ranking Eastman orchestra was simply breathtaking.

Later in 1960, Dr. Fennell and his famous Eastman Wind Ensemble embarked on the giant project of recording the Civil War Centennial album for Mercury Recording. Fennell spent at least four years preparing for this project. He tracked down authentic instruments, located original music books, and made live recordings of gunfire, cannon fire, bugle calls, horses' hooves and other battle sounds associated with the Civil War.

Fennell tuned all the drums for the December recording sessions taking place at the Eastman Theater. He is heard prominently on the recordings performing with the Eastman Percussion Ensemble. The brass recording sessions were completed during the same month. Some of the brass instruments were in pristine condition, while others, especially the larger ones, were in poor condition. Rumor has it that a janitor came into the Annex over the weekend to clean. Spying this pile of what looked like junk, he supposedly threw a considerable number of those banged-up brass instruments into the incinerator where they met their fiery end.

In 1990, PBS produced an eleven-hour television series on the Civil War. Much of the highly acclaimed soundtrack was taken from these Eastman Wind Ensemble recordings of the 1960s.

Jay Berliner

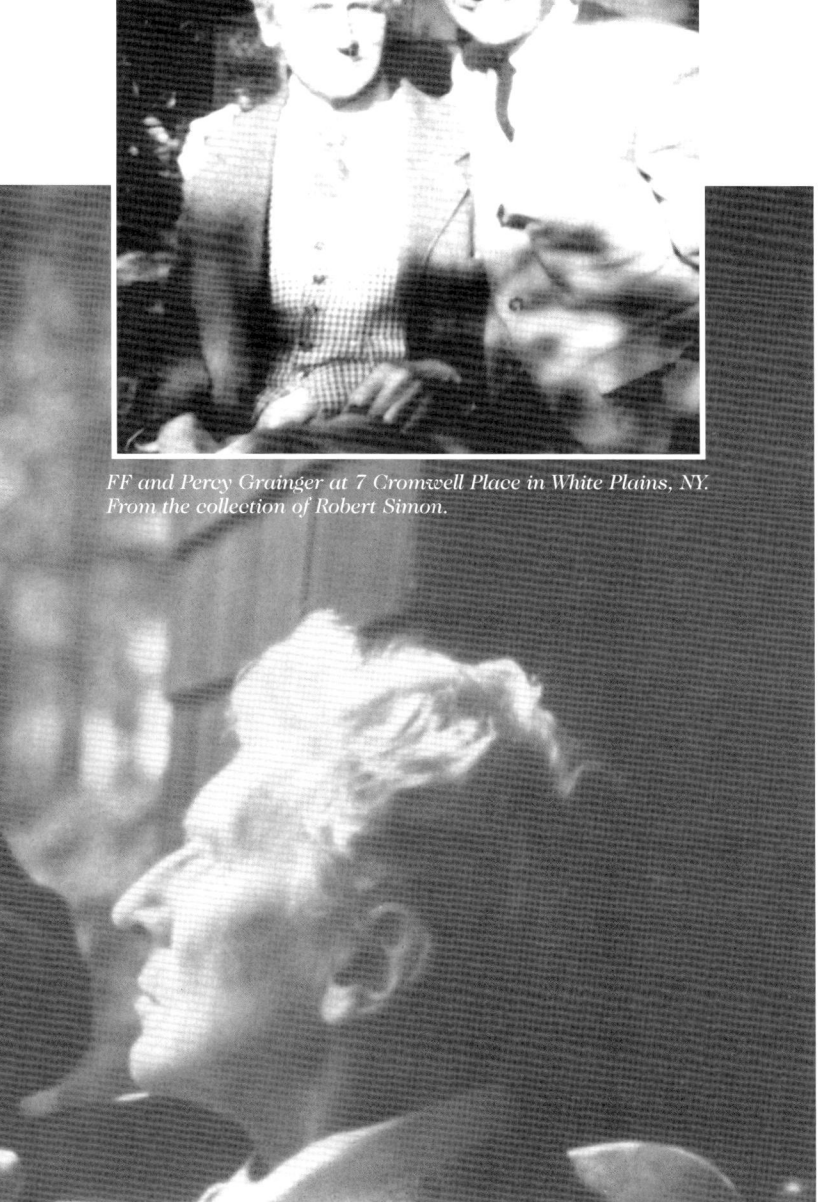

FF and Percy Grainger at 7 Cromwell Place in White Plains, NY. From the collection of Robert Simon.

Frederick Fennell in a Ludwig Drum ad. Courtesy of Bill Ludwig, 1960.

Roger Bobo

As I sit at my computer trying to find the right words to express the enormous impact Frederick Fennell has had on my life, I find myself listening to a recording of *Dionysiaques* by Florent Schmitt, which I performed with Fennell in the late 50s. I knew Dr. Fennell was great back in those days, but in retrospect, I now realize that few of us then really understood the extent of his greatness. Of course, I've played with many great conductors over my tuba career, but those experiences would have been significantly less impressive without the Fennell background.

There are other sides to Frederick Fennell apart from his role as perhaps the greatest ensemble trainer of the past century. Dr. Fennell cared deeply about the well-being of his students; in the eyes of so many of us, he was a kind of "super dad." A personal testimony to his great humanity began shortly after I left Eastman to work with the Concertgebouw Orchestra of Amsterdam. Of course, my time with Concertgebouw and experiences in Europe were exciting, but at the same time, I experienced severe homesickness. Somehow, Dr. Fennell heard about my homesickness and wrote me several letters, which got me through that period.

We all know he is one of the great pedagogues of the twentieth century, but he is so much more.

Roger Bobo
Los Angeles Philharmonic (retired)

David Peter Coppen

During October of 2000, during the triennial Alumni Reunion Weekend of the Eastman School of Music, I was then nearing the end of my second year as Special Collections Librarian and Archivist at the Sibley Music Library. As part of the reunion weekend observance, I had set out old issues of *The Score* (the ESM yearbook) in the Special Collections reading room for returning alumni to enjoy. As I was greeting and chatting with Eastman grads, I noticed a familiar figure reach the top of the stairs outside the Special Collections department.

I had met Maestro Frederick Fennell, during a brief visit to Rochester in November of the previous year. On that occasion, Maestro Fennell had been an honored guest at an Eastman Wind Ensemble concert conducted by Dr. Jim Ripley, who had recently received a Ph.D. in conducting under longtime EWE conductor Dr. Donald Hunsberger. "I'm looking forward to having lunch with you," he told me on the drive from the airport, and after the luncheon, I escorted him back to the Sibley Music Library to examine a wall-length exhibit mounted in the library's Eastman Wind Ensemble room. That exhibit was devoted to Fennell's ten years as EWE director and celebrated the numerous recordings issued in the historic Mercury Living Presence series. Maestro Fennell wrote approvingly of the exhibit when signing the ESM guestbook. More importantly, he paid tribute to the student performers in his inscription. He described his decade as EWE conductor as "a cornucopia of what Eastman student players produced so elegantly and excitingly. It was the players that I so loved making music with that made the difference."

In October of 2000, Maestro Fennell was greeted with visible affection by the numerous alumni gathered there in the Special Collection department. One of them, clearly a former classmate of his, addressed him familiarly as Freddie. After exchanging pleasantries with me, he asked if he might see one of the yearbooks from the 1930s. I guided him towards the "1930s" table and sat down with him, hoping for some of his shared memories.

Turning the pages of the 1934 yearbook, the Maestro paused at length over a photograph of the Freshman Class. He stood out somewhat in the photograph, in part due to his broad smile and boyish good looks, but also due to his attire. Whereas most of the young men in the photograph posed in ties and suits, the young Freddie Fennell looked decidedly more casual in his turtleneck sweater, cuffed slacks, a belt with oversized buckle, and some clunky, Depression-era shoes. "Casual" is too polite a word here. There turned out to be a story behind all of this.

"These were my freshman clothes," the Maestro told me in a thoughtful voice, "they were all I could afford at the time." He particularly commented on the belt and the shoes—all too large and stylistically out of place among his formally attired classmates. As he continued speaking, I received a good idea of the economic imbalances that prevailed during the Depression and how difficult it must have been for a music student living away from home.

Since then, I've opened the 1934 yearbook to that page for many a visitor to the Eastman School. It's difficult not to feel awestruck by the distance the Maestro has travelled. Arriving in Rochester as the undersized drum major from Cleveland, Fennell pulled together the University of Rochester's first-ever marching band. Spurred on by pluck and determination, he earned the Eastman School's first-ever bachelor's degree in applied percussion. Immediately following graduation, Fennell was appointed to the ESM and founded the wind ensemble that has become one of Eastman's grandest success stories. He is beloved the world over and is still in demand for teaching and conducting in his upper 80s.

David Peter Coppen
Special Collections, Sibley Library
Eastman School of Music

Close-up of FF in Freshman Class.

*With 19th-Century horns used in the Civil War recordings.
Photo courtesy of the Eastman School of Music*

Gettysburg, Saturday October 29, 1960. Cannon used in Civil War recording.
Photo by William Decker, courtesy of FF.

*Eastman Philharmonia tour 1961.
Photo courtesy of the Eastman School.*

FF conducts Cole Porter and George Gershwin. Photo by Mary Morris. Courtesy of Universal Polygram.

Robert E. Sheldon

This charming 1961 photo of Dr. Fennell concerns an intersting situation regarding the Eastman School Director, Howard Hanson. Dr. Hanson had enjoyed a long and distinguished career, and he was known to be a master composition teacher capable of reading complex scores at the keyboard. Fully versed in any extreme contemporary style brought to his attention, it did not follow that he therefore wished the more avant-garde composition students to move in those directions. In short, he rather felt that music stylistically should not develop much further out than his own works. It also was clear that he sensed an oncoming obsolescence and being left in the wake of new trends, although they were not all that new in 1961.

Eastman then had a small cult of advanced composition students who pursued styles not appreciated by Dr. Hanson, and they were not very subtle in criticizing his opinions. Dr. Fennell shared our realistic feelings that any style is good and worthy if it is; simple as that. He and roughly a dozen of the Eastman instrumentalists brewed-up a little scheme to put-on the hard core avant-garders with the performance of a supposed new Stockhausen (or similar) work. In fact, neither Stockhausen nor anybody wrote one note of it. We simply ad-libbed an improv "work" for one of the Eastman lunch-time recitals in Kilbourn Hall which often saw the audience body-count similar to that of the performers. But for this performance, the word was out and the avant-garders were there in force, and we later discovered that most of them initially took it quite seriously. With a world-class conductor leading us one would surely have to assume the performance to be quite genuine.

Kilbourn Hall performances usually offered a one-page, octavo size program, and I cannot find my copy (if I managed to keep it from forty-three years ago). The personnel is now a blank. I was the hornist and I vaguely recall that Larry Combs was our clarinetist. Our little mixed string-wind band numbered at least eight players and the Fennell photo shows him leading our rehearsal in the Basement Assembly. Pointillistic lines with constant extremes, including vicious pizzicati, etc. were our goals, and Dr. Fennell instantly developed a set of motions which brought each player, as Percy Grainger would say, "to the fore" with some extreme lick or another. Whatever your instrument was likely to do well "in the style" got the Fennell high sign or low sign. The Fennell acting skills were in high gear as he pretended to keep nose buried in the score to insure an accurate performance of the complex work riddled with the typical unnecessary meter changes. We all had a riotously good-humored time and the performance actually generated some rather good and creative results.

Robert E. Sheldon
ESM 1960

*Frederick Fennell - 1961, Basement Assembly, Eastman School of Music.
Courtesy of Robert E. Sheldon.*

Arrival of the Eastman Philharmonia, Moscow, USSR, January 24, 1962. Notice FF is the only one smiling after the long journey. He is carrying Hanson's briefcase in his right hand and his own score case in his left. On his left lapel is his father's flag pin. Photo courtesy of FF.

Eastman Philharmonia tour to the USSR; 1962, FF as Assistant Conductor alongside Howard Hanson. Some of the orchestra resented Hanson's treatment of FF on this tour. Frederick was opening the concerts with the two National Anthems only. Hanson became too ill to conduct one of the concerts, and FF stepped in at the last minute to do it all. For one of his curtain calls the Philharmonia gave him a long standing ovation! Photo courtesy of the Library of Congress and Robert Sheldon.

Hanson and FF.
Photo courtesy of the Eastman School of Music.

Rehearsal of the Minneapolis Symphony in Northrip Auditorium. Van Cliburn performed Rachmaninoff III and Brahms D minor for a Pension Fund Raiser, February 1963.

Gettysburg, circa 1960s.
Photo courtesy of Universal Polygram.

Listening to playback of Broadway Marches with John Krance (arranger and french hornist) Harold Lawrence and FF, 1964. Photo by Mary Lawrence courtesy of FF.

A familiar photo of FF that was inside the music folders of countless music students with his famous warm-up tips.

Miami Letters

William F. Lee

University of Miami

Two weeks after I arrived in Miami and began my new job as Dean of the School of Music at the University of Miami (September 1964), I recruited Frederick Fennell to become the conducting professor. At the time, Fennell was the Associate Conductor of the Minneapolis Symphony. I learned that he was not happy in that position and might be tempted to migrate south. I directed the Department of Music at Sam Houston State University in Huntsville, 70 miles north of Houston, and I met Fred during his frequent appearances with the Houston Symphony Orchestra in the 50s.

After the traditional visit to the campus and meetings with various members of the administration, Frederick Fennell was offered the position of Professor of Music. After Fennell joined the faculty, I was able to recruit numerous top-notch faculty members partly due to his name and reputation. During Fred's tenure we increased the student enrollment from 150 to 850, making Miami the largest music school at a private university. The faculty also exploded from 20 to 75 full-time members plus several part time positions. Fred retired in 1980.

We both attended many formal concerts, receptions, and such during his fifteen years at the school. However, I recall most vividly an informal occasion in 1967. I, Carl (Doc) Severinsen, Fred, and our respective wives were enjoying cocktails and dinner at the Fennells' home. Doc had just been invited to be the new conductor of the band on the "Tonight Show" and was spending the week with Fred to take private conducting lessons. After dinner, Doc got out his trumpet to warm up; Fred found a phone book and a pair of brushes, and I sat down at the piano. We played a three-hour session on the spot and good times were had by all.

William F. Lee III
Dean of the School of Music,
University of Miami
Executive Vice President/Provost, Emeritus,
University of Miami

Fred Wickstrom

I've known Frederick Fennell as a student under his direction at the University of Illinois ('59), as a faculty colleague at the University of Miami, and as a member of the professional Miami/Florida Philharmonic (1968-1980). I have been energized and educated in all three situations. As a student, I never played for a conductor who was so meticulous about percussion; never before had a conductor placed such demands on me as a snare drummer.

These same demands were placed on my students when he joined me on the faculty of the University of Miami. He taught us things about instrument placement from a conductor's point of view, which stayed with me for the rest of my life. He later incorporated these teachings into a clinic he called "Percussion from the Podium." I blatantly stole that title for some of my own clinics, giving Fred credit every time. I turned the focus of the clinic to what I've learned <u>from</u> conductors <u>on</u> the podium.

To mention a few specifics from his clinics, one must always play the bass drum with the "Fennell Beater," which is a Ludwig marching beater covered with three layers of chamois. One never plays the bass drum with a "mush bag," what he called any other beater, typically those covered in white felt. His insistence on the forty-five-degree tilt of the bass drum with the sound coming off the drum toward the conductor shaped my views on snare and timpani tilt and placement as well. He always directed, "strike the chime straight on not with the hammer at an angle to the tube." Has anyone who's every played under him forgotten the instruction "wait for one"?

Two performances stand out in my mind. The first occurred shortly after Fred joined the faculty at Miami. To say that the school was rebuilding is an understatement. Fred took the student orchestra with a total of twelve string players to a state convention and conducted them with the same verve and passion as if he was conducting the New York Philharmonic. The second was his masterful conducting of Ives's *Fourth Symphony* with the Miami/Florida Philharmonic. His careful attention to detail made it so much easier for us, the orchestra, to get through a very difficult score.

Perhaps the greatest thing any of us got from Fred was a passion for making music. He increased mine and for that I'm eternally grateful.

Fred Wickstrom
University of Miami, Percussion Program Director

William Lee, Aaron Copland, Clifton Williams and Frederick Fennell, University of Miami, 1967.

William Klinger

For many years I was the professor of clarinet at the University of Miami School of Music. During a portion of those years, Frederick Fennell was the conductor of the University Symphony Orchestra and wind ensemble. I believe he also served as chairman of the Applied Music Department. We had a comfortable working relationship.

One day, he called me into his office and said, "Bill, The MENC (Music Educators National Conference) is being held in Miami later this year and I'd like you to play the Alvin Etler *Concerto* with the Wind Ensemble." I said, "Great, when is it?" He gave me the date and I told him I couldn't because I was, "Playing the Symphony." I could see he was upset, which was understandable, but when he asked about the next day and I told him I couldn't because I was, "Playing the Opera," his temperature really began to rise. Finally, he asked about the day following that and when I said I couldn't because I was "Playing the Ballet," it was just too much. In a state of semi-apoplexy he blurted out, "For Gods' sake, is there anything you don't play?" My response was, "Yes, saxophone!" I'll leave his reaction up to the imagination of the reader.

William Klinger
Professor Emeritus
University of Miami
School of Music

With Byron Janis performing Rachmaninoff's III with the Greater Miami Philharmonic, November, 1974.

Bob Parker

When I joined the University of Miami School of Music faculty in 1972, Fred Fennell headed the Instrumental Music Department and conducted both the UM Wind Ensemble and the Symphony Orchestra. There was solid support for the instrumental program. Two renowned wind ensemble composers, Clifton Williams and Alfred Reed, were on the faculty. The wind and percussion professors, drawn mainly from the Miami (now the Florida) Philharmonic, included New York Philharmonic alumnus Harry Glantz. Jerry Coker and Gerry Miligan were stalwarts in the jazz faculty for a brief period. Dean William Lee was building a strong and balanced school of music, and, with the administrative assistance of Graduate Studies Director, Neal Glenn (my own mentor in graduate administration), attracted a number of top graduate students and teaching assistants. Oswald Award-winning composer Lawrence Weiner was Clifton Williams's student and teaching assistant; his sterling dissertation composition was performed by Fennell's Wind Ensemble. Woodwind specialist Peter Vollmers was Fennell's teaching assistant, as well as a promising conductor and composer. The orchestra was good, but Fennell's abilities as a wind ensemble specialist shone most brilliantly. His concerts attracted large and enthusiastic audiences who relished his learned commentaries as well as the music itself.

Bob Parker
University of Miami

Paul F. Edgar

I graduated from the University of Miami with a Bachelor's degree in Music Education in January of 1971. I performed in the University Orchestra and Wind Ensemble as a percussionist and timpanist. Upon arriving as a freshman, I was very inexperienced in the world of concert percussion. Most of my experience had been on drum set. Dr. Fennell seemed able to tell this and he was on my case, rightfully so, for the next two semesters. I made considerable progress during my first year. I started to gain his confidence and respect, which led to my becoming section leader in the Orchestra and Wind Ensemble. Only a few of the percussion majors were allowed this position. I even managed to play timpani in the Orchestra and, my crowning moment, in the Wind Ensemble. However, I have several stories about the road to such success with Dr. Fennell.

At one point as a freshman, Aaron Copland was to come to conduct a piece called *Emblems* for wind ensemble. The piece called for extensive use of percussion. Not being aware that Dr. Fennell's instrument was, in fact, percussion, I was not prepared for what was about to happen. I was not ready to perform at the level that Dr. Fennell required. I made every mistake in the book, including instruments rolling off a table clattering to the floor. After the first rehearsal, in front of the entire wind ensemble, he told the percussion section that if we were unprepared for the next rehearsal he would see us all thrown out of the School of Music and the University. He made special remarks directed personally at me. For example, he requested that I use a certain color of mallet on a wood block. I, of course, did not have this particular mallet. He said, "Don't come to the next rehearsal without the proper equipment." I had others, which were almost as hard as the ones he wanted, but mine were a different color. By the next rehearsal, I had not obtained the correct mallets, but I figured he couldn't really see the mallets I was using and since they were so close in hardness it would be alright. After three notes, he stopped and said, "Those are not the mallets I requested, I told you, 'Musser Blues,' get out of my rehearsal!" After several sleepless nights, I was able to get through rehearsals without incident. The concert went fine. Later that year, Dr. Fennell mentioned to me that it looked like I might make it through the rest of the year.

Later that same year, the Orchestra played a concert off-campus. There was almost no percussion demanded by the program and as the only freshman in the group, I was elected to go. On one piece, an opera aria, there was a single bass drum note, to be played very softly. Like the jerk I was at the time, I asked, "Since the bass drum is used only this once should we even bother to bring the drum at all." The look on his face told me the answer, but he answered verbally as well: "Mr Edgar, have you translated the words of the singer just before your entrance?" "It means 'dead,'" he said, "and your bass drum note sets the tone of the last sentence the singer performs." Even worse, I missed the note in the concert, even though he cued me perfectly. One can imagine the words he saved for me after the show.

While these two anecdotes seem to suggest Dr. Fennell's impatience, they, in fact, speak to his demand for musical excellence at all times. Upon graduation, Dr. Fennell told me how proud he was to have me in his ensembles and thanked me for the outstanding progress and contributions that I had made. Finally, he told me I had achieved his level of performance. I almost cried.

Since my college days, I have been a professional musician for thirty years. I played in the US Navy Band, Washington, D.C., the Kennedy Opera House Orchestra, had extra status with the National Symphony Orchestra, and I have been involved in just about every other aspect of the Washington musical scene for the past twenty-five years. I have also been the head of the percussion department at George Washington University for the last nineteen years. As a freelance musician, I have used the concepts and discipline that Dr. Fennell taught me. My success has been entirely his doing. I would never have reached my present status without his early guidance, even though it was painful at times. I love this man dearly. He is truly the most importance influence in my musical life.

Paul F. Edgar

Some of the Maestro's scores, which include his edits and notes. Courtesy of Kosei Publishing, photo by Kawamura.

A familiar photo of FF that was inside the music folders of countless music students with his famous warm-up tips and "LISTEN." Also shown on page 96.

FF is on the podium at University of Miami. Courtesy of the Music Department of the University of Miami at Coral Gables, FL, and Nicholas DeCarbo.

FF Impressions

Frank Battisti

I have known Fred since 1953, the year I began teaching in the Ithaca (NY) City School District. Fred had just started the Eastman Wind Ensemble (1952). He quickly became the kind of conductor I wanted to be, and the Eastman Wind Ensemble became the model I wanted to develop to teach my students music. Since Ithaca was only 90 miles from Rochester, I began taking my band students to Eastman Wind Ensemble concerts. Often after a concert, Fred would come out to our tour bus and talk to the students, thanking them for coming to the concert.

Fred was also involved in numerous activities with my band. Every year on the day before Memorial Day, Fred would spend the day rehearsing the band. Each year the repertoire consisted of pieces that Fred had recorded with the Eastman Wind Ensemble and pieces that we had heard at Eastman concerts. The students were always well prepared, making it possible for Fred to work his "magic" on them. This was always the highlight of the year for us.

There was never a public performance associated with his visits, just a wonderful day of music making followed by an equally wonderful banquet. These banquets always included the presentation of a gift to the Maestro. The gift had to be unique. The students felt that a traditional gift would not adequately express their admiration, appreciation, love, and respect. One of their most interesting and unusual gifts was a deed from the United States Department of the Interior making Fred owner of eight square feet of the Gettysburg battlefield. A national campaign was underway to save the battlefield from developers, the students knew of Fred's interest in Civil War history and music. They decided to purchase a small part of the battlefield to give to Fred. He was thrilled to become part owner of this sacred ground, and the students were happy to once again surprise and please their beloved guest conductor.

Over the years, Fred appeared as a guest conductor with every ensemble I have directed, including Ithaca High School, Baldwin Wallace Symphonic Wind Ensemble, and the New England Conservatory Wind Ensemble. I consider Fred one of the finest people I have ever known, and he is the person most responsible for the musician and person I have become.

Frank Battisti
New England Conservatory

From the office of Frank Battisti at Ithica High School in 1963.

*Rehearsal, Interlochen 1967-1969.
Photo courtesy of Interlochen Center for the Arts.*

Harvey G. Phillips

Dr. Frederick Fennell has long been established as a major force in twentieth-century music and beyond. His influence on musicians of his own generation and future generations is well-documented and recorded. In the middle of the twentieth century, Frederick Fennell defined and championed wind ensemble instrumentation and compiled a repertoire of enormous variety, quality and quantity by researching, transcribing, commissioning, inspiring, charming and cajoling composers. Through countless live concerts and an unprecedented series of successful commercial recordings, he established the professional wind ensemble and elevated it to the top rank of college and conservatory performing ensembles. By example, he inspired an army of loyal disciples, many of whom have advanced to important professional and academic positions. The significance of Dr. Frederick Fennell's achievements as a musician, educator, and conductor cannot be measured but assuredly ranks him with such famous predecessors as John Philip Sousa and Edwin Franko Goldman.

For many years, I have enjoyed a personal and professional association with Dr. Frederick Fennell. I have performed under his direction at numerous music conventions and on other occasions, including a commercial recording entitled *Broadway Marches*. I appreciate the many years of his unwavering endorsement and support of my various and sundry activities to elevate the status of my instrument: the tuba.

On numerous occasions, at my request, he has volunteered to conduct Merry Tuba Christmas concerts, started in 1974 to honor my teacher, the late great William Bell; through him, these concerts pay tribute to all the great artists and teachers of tuba and euphonium. Also on these occasions, we gratefully acknowledge composers who have embraced our instruments with their solo and ensemble compositions through American composer Alec Wilder. Wilder arranged the Christmas music performed by our mass tuba/euphonium choirs. Fred, also a close friend of Alec Wilder and an admirer of Bill Bell, was among the first to conduct Tuba Christmas concerts. When Fred's schedule permitted, he often toured with me to New York City, Washington, D.C., Chicago, Dallas, and Los Angeles. Many friends visited with us in each city, and hundreds of tuba and euphonium players of all ages have been excited to perform with the famous Dr. Frederick Fennell. One year we were in Los Angeles and Dr. Carl L. Randolph—president of United States Borax Corporation, vice-chairman of the Harvey Phillips Foundation, and himself a fine tubist—invited us to dinner at his home in Huntington Beach. After a wonderful dinner, we boarded the Randolph's yacht and toured the harbor and inlets of Huntington Beach, enjoying traditional and spectacular Christmas decorations. Each year, Fred, in spite of a demanding schedule, somehow reserves time to rehearse and conduct our traditional Merry Tuba Christmas Chicago in the lobby of the Palmer House Hilton Hotel. He wears his special Tuba Christmas attire, and some 400 tuba and euphonium players of all ages are thrilled to perform under his direction. Dr. Frederick Fennell continues to be generous with his enormous talent and boundless energy; his legacy will most assuredly continue to enrich the lives of future generations.

Harvey G. Phillips

Guest conductors Peter J. Wilhousky, Sir Vivian Dunn of Her Majesty's Marines, interim Interlochen President George C. Wilson and FF, 1971. Courtesy Interlochen Center for the Arts.

Frederick Fennell getting the bass drum just perfect during rehearsal on authentic 19th-century instruments as used in recording for "The Civil War–Its Music and Its Sound." Courtesy of Robert E. Sheldon, photo by Jon Newsom.

Engaged as a bass drummer and conductor for a 19th-century band project. Photo by Jon Newsom, and courtesy of Robert Sheldon.

Rehearsal with the EWE in 1974. Photo by Louis Ouzer.

Sir David Whitwell

The most important, and revealing, moments of my long friendship with Fred involve things which must remain personal.

However, I can recall several occasions involving scores which I knew well, indeed scores which I had rehearsed and performed from memory, when I then heard a performance by Fred which left me stunned and embarrassed in the revealed truths I had not perceived. While others, on this occasion, will point to his remarkable recording career, his unique fluency in speaking and writing, and his engaging personality, for me it has always been the depth of pure musicianship in Fred's conducting which has been the most impressive.

Sir David Whitwell

Rehearsal with the EWE in 1974 - Louis Ouzer

Alfred Reed

Looking back over a period of some 53 years now, it seems to me that the course of our future relationship, both professional and personal during this time, was set almost from our first meeting in person, after some preliminary correspondence dealing with his interest in performing my *Russian Christmas Music* with the Eastman Wind Ensemble.

After Frederick had rented the material for the *Russion Christmas Music* and had rehearsed it, he wrote to me and said that he anticipated it would be a "sensational success at the performance" and, as I was later to be informed, that is indeed what it turned out to be. And several weeks later I had the opportunity of meeting him for the first time in person, when he came to New York on a trip to see some people he told me he felt he must see and talk to.

He pointed out to me, after we had listened to a sort of medium-fi tape that was the best that could be done half a century ago, and played on what could have been no more than a low-fi tape player, that he felt obliged to add a few notes in one or two of the percussion parts in the final section that he felt would add even more excitement and color to the sound of the music at that point (he was right, too). And we talked for about an hour about future plans on my part and his as regards wind music that gave me the opportunity to see how devoted he was to his branch of the musical art, how seriously he took it, and how convinced he was as to the merits of such a position.

To me it was obvious that he was indeed a driven man, solidly rooted in a love for music, and determined to pursue his dream of having wind music recognized beyond the borders of marches, polkas and waltzes, which was really all that "bands" were deemed suited for and capable of. This, to my mind, required a special kind of personal and professional courage at the time, because the prevailing attitude in the musical profession could well be summarized by a slight alteration in Shakespeare's lines in "Romeo and Juliet" where Juliet says, "A rose by any other name would smell as sweet," to read, "What's in a name? A band by any other name would sound the same!"

But the fact impressed itself on me with great urgency that in listening to what Frederick had done with Wind Ensemble in the matter of purity of instrumental color, balance among wood and brass, dexterity and clarity of whatever texture the music might consist of, and complete adaptability to any kind or type of music was really the first time I had ever heard this in reality, outside of hearing it in my imagination, in "ever-lovin'-livin'-blue-eyed-technicolor sound" (as Pogo used to say in the old comic strip). That first-time experience made me realize fully and completely that it COULD indeed be done. Which, in turn, convinced me that what I might even have regarded as an impossible dream: namely that the wind orchestra and the symphony orchestra could indeed be the opposite sides of the same coin, to be called "serious large-scale music for large-scale instrumental performing groups" was not only possible, but it existed.

This realization changed my musical life, and set me on the road to whatever I may have accomplished to date.

Alfred Reed

*Eastman Wind Ensemble with FF as guest conductor, 1974.
Photo courtesy of the Eastman School of Music.*

Rehearsal at Interlochen 1975. Photo courtesy of Interlochen Center for the Arts.

Earle Dhus

I would like to relate a small incident, with large implications about the mind and character of the great human being Frederick Fennell. In May 1955, I was a seventeen-year-old clarinetist at the Pennsylvania State Band, which took place in Alliquippa. While there were no auditions at the State Band level, Fennell held auditions for the clarinet section, and I managed to land the position of soloist for a piece called *From Africa to Harlem*.

It just so happened that my senior prom took place on the same night as the concert. The prom was in Erie, PA, some 150 miles from the location of the concert. My date was my steady girl, whom I later married. (Over forty years later, we have three grown children and four grandchildren). Thus, the event was very important to me, and I sensed this even then. I had already arranged for a flight back to Erie that evening so I could make the last few hours of the prom, but it meant that I would miss the last half of the concert. A problem developed when I saw *From Africa to Harlem* on the second half of the program.

In my seventeen-year-old ignorance and arrogance, I walked up to Dr. Fennell without any statement of a problem, without any indication what I was talking about, and said, "I can't be here for the second half of the concert." That was all I said. In less than one second, he recognized me from the other 250 band members and remembered that I was to play that little solo in *From Africa to Harlem*. Very significantly, he did not question my reasons for not being able to play the second half, and he solved the problem. He simply moved the piece to the first half of the program.

It was many years before I realized what had taken place in that brief two sentence exchange. I had teenagers of my own by then and had finally begun to understand something of the greatness of Frederick Fennell as a person and musician. As I reflect on this small moment in my early life, I now realize that I was in the presence of someone rare and special.

Earle Dhus

Robert Klotman, Howard Hanson, FF and Glenn Block, 1977. Photo courtesy of Interlochen Center for the Arts.

David Hall

In the spring of 1959, Fred paid my wife and I a visit in Wilton Connecticut. Together we attended the annual Muster of Ancient Martial Music Festival featuring fife-and-drum and drum-and-bugle corps from all over the region. We heard traditional marching tunes and drum figures executed on authentic instruments. There were huge, cylindrical bass drums played with potato masher sticks and wooden fifes. It was a thoroughly enjoyable time for all, and I like to think that this experience influenced Fred's later work with Civil War music and history.

David Hall

Ron Friedman

In 1961, I was in the All Eastern Conference High School Band, and Frederick Fennell was the guest conductor. My first impression was of a short, elven man wrapping his watch and pocket contents into a handkerchief and giving it to the principal flute. However, his appearance was quickly over-shadowed by his extraordinary memory. He got up on the podium without a score and began rehearsing the Persichetti *Symphony for Band*. He called out performance comments by instrument and measure number. For instance, "second trumpet, hold the F in measure twenty-two for full value." Again, he never cracked a score.

Thirty-eight years later, I was eating in a Baltimore restaurant near the concert hall, and Maestro Fennell was eating at the next table. He was in town to conduct the United States Marine Band that evening. As he rose to leave, I introduced myself, explaining that I had been in the MENC group all those years ago. He said, "Great! We're playing the same piece tonight." Sure enough, the Persichetti Symphony was on the program—Great memory.

Ron Friedman

*During a celebration weekend honoring members of the Eastman Wind Ensemble at the Eastman School.
Photo courtesy of Louis Ouzer, 1977.*

Paul D. Parkman

When I was a junior at Weedsport Central School, I had the good fortune to go to All State Band in Rochester. Our conductor there was Frederick Fennell. I played first horn with enthusiasm but not a great deal of skill. The music that Dr. Fennell chose for our concert was more difficult than anything I had ever played before. During the first day's rehearsal, he thoroughly rehearsed the same difficult passage, telling us exactly how it should sound. We were worried that we would never get to the rest of the program; we finally did, but only on the second day.

One piece was especially hard for us. It seemed very modern and atonal with odd meters, which he had to train us to count. He wanted the drummers to play loudly. Their drum strokes were to mimic pistol shots, he said, as he dramatically shouted "Banzai," slumped, and twisted on the podium as if shot. He said that for every head they broke he would buy them two new ones.

On the evening of the concert, the auditorium filled and we bravely began. All went well until we got to the last piece: the "Banzai" piece. The trumpet section, responsible for the main melody, got irretrievably lost and sat in despondent, adolescent silence while the rest of us labored to the end. After polite applause, the crowd rose to leave, but Dr. Fennell turned to them and asked, "wouldn't you like to hear that last piece again?" We sat down, played it again, and everybody kept their place. How kind he was.

Paul D. Parkman, M.D.

Dr. Thomas L. Mentzer

I played under Frederick Fennell during my Penn State days at the Pennsylvania All-Collegiate band festival in Westminster College. We were rehearsing the band arrangement of Dvořák's *New World Symphony*. An extended crescendo passage built interminably to a fortissimo fermata, and Dr. Fennell milked it for all it was worth. While he stood there, arms outstretched, an inattentive trumpet player destroyed the mood by making the next entry long before Dr. Fennell was ready. The conductor looked as though he had been shot! Still holding the fermata pose, he toppled forward, crashing into the flute section. Sitting in the clarinet section, I thought that he must have had a heart attack right there in front of us. Instead, he climbed up over the flute players' shoulders and looked aghast at the offending trumpeter. All he said was "don't EVER do that again." Needless to say, that passage was flawless in the concert.

Dr. Thomas L. Mentzer
Chairman of Psychology, University of New Haven

Anne Lutz

In 1962, I had the pleasure of playing piccolo and flute in the All-County Senior Band concert in Schoharie County, New York. Three rehearsals took place for our Saturday night performance. Dr. Fennell couldn't be there for the first rehearsal and things did not go well with the substitute conductor. However, Dr. Fennell took over and won our hearts. He was personable, entertaining, funny, inspiring, and we knew, from the first moment, that he as a great conductor. We were impressed with his short stature and the fact that he used a stool to sit on during rehearsal, sometimes conducting with his feet, and occasionally standing on it when he wanted the group to play loud. Every time we stopped playing, he had something interesting or funny to tell us. He had just returned from a trip abroad with the Eastman School Orchestra and told us how surprised the people in Moscow were at the youthfulness of the musicians. He also told us that he would much rather conduct a group like us than be in Moscow. He inspired us to play, in our minds, "perfectly"; we took up a collection and bought him a rather expensive traveling case, because we were so pleased with what we accomplished under his leadership.

To this day, I remember the wonderful experience of that weekend, and I remember fondly that he was so kind to a group of high schoolers in a small rural county in upstate New York. Thank you, Dr. Fennell.

Anne Lutz

Kenneth Pick

In 1966, I was a young college tubist in the Fredonia Wind Ensemble (State University College, Fredonia, New York). The legendary Dr. Frederick Fennell was to come down from nearby Eastman and guest conduct Robert Russell Bennett's *Suite of Old American Dances*. The brief rehearsal went well as we were all well prepared. The concert was memorable.

Fred showed up in a blue-and-white striped seersucker suit; we were all in concert attire. As we approached one of the more rhythmical movements with intricate syncopations, Fred conducted the more lyrical melody heard in the piccolo, flute, and clarinet. The whole back row of low brass and percussion looked up in amazement, fully expecting a crisp, definitive beat pattern—something to hang our hat on. We were holding on for dear life. In my young career, this experience taught me what was truly important in a piece of music. Also, his attire gave us insight into the person; he was not a stuffed shirt but a real person with a great sense of humor.

Throughout my career as a middle-school band director, I have tried to remember these two lessons: always conduct that which is important, and don't take yourself too seriously.

Kenneth Pick

Rehearsal at Interlochen, 1978.
Photo courtesy Interlochen Center for the Arts.

Wayne Asbury

In 1966 as a sophomore oboist, I auditioned and was accepted to the All-State Honor Band here in California. After chair tryouts, I was placed as seventh out of eight oboe players. I played in the concert band. I was disappointed not to make the top band, but I knew I might have a chance in succeeding years. I did have the opportunity to sit in on some of their rehearsals and I was immediately in awe of the conductor. I learned that the man's name was Frederick Fennell. I had no clue who that was.

I went home and practiced even harder and made the top band the next year (1967) as a junior. I got to play under Frederick Fennell. I was in music heaven for weeks.

My senior year in high school, I was privileged to play principal oboe in the California All-State Band. Frederick Fennell was our guest conductor for a third consecutive year. We were rehearsing the "Ballet of the Unhatched Chicks" from *Pictures at an Exhibition* by Moussorgsky. There is a very difficult oboe solo in the middle and when we came to it, I was very nervous. It went flawlessly, (at least in the mind of a 17-year-old). After I had finished Fennell turned to me and said, "Young man! This is not an oboe concerto! This is the 'Ballet of Unhatched Chicks.' So!!! PLAY LIKE A CHICKEN!" From then on, I PLAYED LIKE A CHICKEN. I have also been known to play like a DUCK.

Another story of this great man was related to me by one of my oboe teachers. He was the son of a band director, if I remember correctly, somewhere in Arizona. They were one of the host families for members of an Honors Band for the weekend. He had gone out late one night during the honor band stay and came home late. So not to disturb the household, he decided to go around the back of the house and sneak in. He climbed through his bedroom window and landed directly on, guess whom?— Frederick Fennell. He had no idea his bedroom had been given away to the notable guest for the weekend.

Wayne Asbury
Lompac, CA
Principal Oboist
San Luis Obispo Symphony
Band and Orchestra Director, Lompoc Valley Middle School

FF at Interlochen Music Camp, 1976. Photo courtesy Jeannette Dowd Hurlburt.

John Whitney

As a high school junior in 1959, I'd heard about Fred before I met him. My dad, Maurice, who was a public school teacher and was active in NYSSMA circles, knew Dr. Fennell. Fred conducted the NY All-State Orchestra in 1959, and I scraped along on second violin for a memorable performance. I adored every moment of rehearsals and wept after the concert, which was at the Concord Hotel. Through my work at Ithaca HS in 1966-67, I came to know and share Frank Battisti's reverence for Fred's work.

In the summer of 1968, I was invited to join a few students on a trip to the International Music Festival at Daytona Beach. The institute there, partially sponsored by Stetson University, hosted a full orchestra during the four-week visit of the London Symphony Orchestra. Our conductor was Geoffrey Gilbert, formerly principal flutist with Beecham. He had a wealth of knowledge about the repertoire. Andre Previn conducted us in *Billy the Kid*, and that summer was the first that Previn, Ashkenazy, and Perlman came to know each other and make music together.

Dr. Fennell also conducted the LSO in a concert or two and was scheduled to conduct the final Tchaikovsky program of the combined groups in the Daytona Beach Jai-Alai Fronton. The finale was to feature the massed groups playing 1812. For those readers uninitiated in Jai-Alai, the playing venues are like theaters with a huge stage. The crowd is protected by a large "curtain" of chicken wire, which keeps the fast moving ball under control. The front third of the "stage" is hardwood and the rest is made of concrete.

The LSO's fourth chair violinist was a great jokester and was always ready with a quip or sight gag, delivered in classic, droll, British style. During the rehearsal of the finale, he removed a strip of firecrackers from his case (at the appropriate moment) and lit one, attempting to toss it on the cement portion of the floor. Hilarity ensued as the jokester dropped the firecracker into his own case and the rest of the package ignited. The firecrackers caused a terrible clatter, singeing the beautiful felt of his case and burning though the horsehair of his spare bow. In the chaos that followed, Fred could only join in the laughter, but he was as surprised as everyone else.

FF at Interlochen. Courtesy of the Instrumentalist Company.

I've seen Fred several times in the past four decades. However, the last time, December of 2000, was the most memorable. Watching him conduct the Eastman Wind Ensemble, I knew I wasn't the only one weeping. The memories, values, and great music provided by a legendary music educator to two generations of students proved too strong for emotion to deny.

John Whitney

The Cleveland Symphonic Winds, Severance Hall, set and players for Handel's Music for the Royal Fireworks. Second day's session for the Telarc Digital recording, April 5, 1978.

Cover of a Cleveland Winds digital recording featuring Arnaud, Vaughan Williams and Grainger by Telarc. Photo courtesy of Jack Renner, Telarc.

Helen Chelengarian-Greene

I was a student at Tanglewood one summer and played in the Symphony Orchestra conducted by Frederick Fennell. After several rehearsals, he announced the audition date for a Concertmaster who would play solo violin in the concert. The number was Rimsky-Korsakov's *Scheherazade*.

I practiced this unfamiliar piece long and hard; I won the position, though I was young without much orchestral experience. I've always been grateful that Frederick Fennell gave me the opportunity to perform solos as well as get experience as a Concertmaster. Frederick Fennell has a gift for picking challenging music for his concerts and a great talent for pushing his performers to new heights of musical beauty.

Cover of the first Cleveland Winds recording by Telarc. Photo courtesy of Jack Renner, Telarc.

Helen Chelengarian-Greene
Boston Musicians' Association

Cliff Johnson

I played bass with the Minneapolis Symphony/Minnesota Orchestra from 1948 to 1999. Freddie joined us in the 1960s. He enjoyed touring in the smoker bus, and we enjoyed his company. Freddie Fennell was the Minneapolis Symphony Assistant Conductor for a season or two. He seemed interested in the smoking pipes that I carved. Our friends from Minneapolis, Don and Barbara Hansen, had most of their kids in All State Band one year. Fennell was the guest conductor and lecturer that year. Don and Barb were in the school kitchen when Fred came in for a drink of water. Don was smoking a large pipe I had carved for him. It had a duck carved on the side of the bowl. Freddie said, "There's only one man who would carve a pipe like that! Cliff Johnson." They were stunned.

Cliff Johnson

David Winer

I first encountered Dr. Frederick Fennell when I was a high school senior. I had the opportunity to perform under Dr. Fennell as the tubist in the Massachusetts All-State Orchestra in 1973. I remember going up to him at the end of one rehearsal just after I had learned that I had been rejected for admission to the Eastman School of Music. He said to me (paraphrased): "You're a good player—don't give up. Eastman had over 50 tuba applicants this year, for only two openings."

Playback during a Telarc digital recording session. Dr. Thomas Stockham, Jack Renner and F.F. Stockham virtually invented this digital recording process. Jack Renner and Robert Woods brought it to market as Telarc Digital. This changed the face of recorded music and FF was the director at the start of the digital era. Photo courtesy of Jack Renner, Telarc.

I had not given up. I graduated from The New England Conservatory in Tuba and Music Education. In 1986, as a young band director in Portland, Maine, I was fortunate to be part of an organization that brought Dr. Fennell to Portland for a full week's stay. Using my school as a base, we brought in three bands a day. In addition, Fred directed rehearsals and a joint concert, featuring my select regional wind ensemble (Portland Youth Wind Ensemble), the local community band, (People's – now Casco Bay – Community Band), and the University of Southern Maine Wind Ensemble. At the end of the week, Dr. Fennell conducted our Regional Band at the Festival, for which I was the Band Chairman. During the week, Dr. Fennell must have conducted over fifty works, yet he never looked at a score. He just asked me, "OK, David, what's this band playing?"

Technical consultant and mastering engineer Stan Ricker listening to a digital playback. Photo courtesy of Telarc.

He got up on the podium and went to work; he knew every note, every rehearsal marking, nuance, dynamic, style marking. Amazing!

More than a decade later, I attended a conducting workshop at the University of Connecticut, where Jeffrey Renshaw has made Frederick Fennell a regular visitor. After having reintroduced myself to Dr. Fennell, he promptly declared, "Portland, Maine!" What a memory!

Recently, I had the pleasure of attending the luncheon to honor my mentor and inspiration, Frank Battisti, and my alma mater, The New England Conservatory. Of the many icons of our profession who were in attendance, the most prominent was, of course, Dr. Fennell. Now we're on a first-name basis: he's "Dr. Fennell," and I'm "Portland, Maine."

David Winer
Avon High School, Avon, Connecticut

Jennifer Martin

I first met Dr. Fennell in 1976. I was a student at California State University, Fullerton, and Fred conducted a session at the Wind Ensemble National Conference at Cal. State Northridge. Because I started collecting famous wind-ensemble recordings while still in high school, he already lived as a hero to me.

I got to know Fred better during 1977-84 when I studied at the West Coast Conducting Symposium at Saddleback College in Mission Viejo, Ca. Fred came nearly every summer and shared wonderful weeks with us. He taught us about resistance by conducting legato while in the swimming pool. We had thrilling talks about Percy Grainger, the Eastman years, sailing, and the state of the musical world.

Over the years, Fred has been so very gracious with his time, friendship, and unsurpassed knowledge. So many personal correspondences and telephone calls between us are cherished mementos for me. A copy of the sign that simply says "LISTEN," which hung in the Eastman School rehearsal room for so long, now proudly adorns my rehearsal hall.

At the University of Calgary, in the summer of 1991, Fred told me that Don Hunsberger was organizing a fortieth anniversary celebration of the founding of the Eastman Wind Ensemble. That night over a beer, Fred said, "You just have to be there." I was so thrilled when I arrived in Rochester that February. I was going to conduct the Eastman Wind Ensemble thanks to the Conductors' Guild. Upon arrival, I sought out the famed Eastman Theater. I just had to be in the room where all of those glorious recording were made and where so much wonderful music was, and is, produced. I walked through the backstage door and found the hall was dark except for the safety light on the stage. I stood there for a long time soaking it all in. Through the darkness, I heard footsteps and turned to see Fred accompanied by Toru Miura, euphonium soloist of the Kosei Wind Orchestra. Fred and I hugged, and he said, "This is where it all happened. Enjoy!" It's a memory I'll always cherish. In February of 2002, I happily returned to Rochester for the EWE's fiftieth anniversary celebration, again organized by Don Hunsberger. Fred was there, of course, moving a little more slowly for sure, but still full of wisdom, wit, and warmth.

Jennifer Martin
Conductor/Professor of Music
Truckee Meadows Community College

FF recording with the Cleveland Winds. Photo courtesy of Telarc.

Brian Jones

As a member of both the Wind Ensemble at the University of North Texas and the Symphonic Band at Indiana University, I was privy to Dr. Fennell's transcendental musicianship twice. His guest appearances were absolute revelations. Under Dr. Fennell's baton, we were more aware of each other as an ensemble, more observant of note lengths, and we all had a ball. He seems to have that rare combination of hot and cold, in that he possesses both the love and feel of music and the consummate technical expertise to transmit it to an ensemble and audience. I feel a huge debt of gratitude to him.

A memory that sticks out to me occurred at North Texas State. I was a member of a marching drum-line that was a perennial national champion. That year, we found ourselves at the Texas Music Educators Association as clinicians. At the same convention, Dr. Fennell was a guest on the podium in our school's wind ensemble concert. Dr. Fennell happened to pass by as the drum-line was warming up outdoors. We recognized him, of course, and stopped to pay our respects to a great musician and conductor who we knew had grown up a drummer.

In the course of our meeting, we realized that the arrangement of Bernstein's overture to *Candide*, which we were to perform in an hour, was arranged according to the same measure-for-measure structure as the original. Suddenly it hit us, and in our hubris we didn't hesitate to ask Dr. Fennell if he would conduct us in *Candide*. It speaks volumes about the man's sense of adventure that he did not hesitate in accepting our invitation. He proceeded to lead us through the overture, marching moves and all. We never played it so well, and the signature micro-coda that we added to the end made him double over with laughter.

Once in awhile, I hear a wonderful sounding wind ensemble on a classical music station and know it's an old Eastman recording before the announcer acknowledges it as such. Dr. Fennell's import is truly that strong. I'll never forget him.

Brian Jones
Principal Timpanist, Detroit Symphony Orchestra

FF portrait, circa early 1980s.

*Recording in Severance Hall with the Cleveland Winds.
Courtesy of Telarc, photo by Nat Silverman.*

Michael Bookspan

Frederick Fennell's contributions to music are so far-reaching and important, that we sometimes forget that he is a wonderful listener and a superb audience. At a musicale that I gave at our Florida condo, Fred would leap to his feet and say something like "That was terrific Mickey" and generated such enthusiasm, that the 35 or so people there, including both musicians and music lovers, caught that energy and a good time was had by all. I'll never forget that experience.

Michael Bookspan
Principal Percussion,
Philadelphia Orchestra

1982, teaching harmonia to young David Anderson, the son of the Eastman clarinet graduate, William Anderson, class of 1963. Bill wrote, "I think these pictures capture his extraordinary 'humanness.'" Bill Anderson, Professor of Music, Kent State University.

Gregor Pierce

I played in the California All-State Band all four years in the late 1970s. In the last two years, I was first chair. I played under Fennell a few times with that group and an experience we shared remains vividly with me today.

It was near the end of nine hours rehearsing on a Saturday night. We were playing a slow movement of a piece by Vincent Persichetti. As we started, I noticed that my part was mostly an ostinato. I decided not to look at my music and to focus on the conductor for as long as possible. As we played, I deeply felt the beautiful music. Frederick Fennell noticed that I was not using the music and he started looking back at me: eye to eye. I could tell that he was enjoying the music as well, and as he conducted the piece and gave cues to the other musicians, his eyes never left mine. As the movement went on, so did this connection. On the last phrase of the movement, I quickly looked down at the music and back at him, but the connection had ended.

In over twenty years of performing since that evening, I have never had such a long, warm, and intense feeling with a conductor. I believe that the spirit of Persichetti, Fennell, and I were embraced in a way that enhances life.

Gregor Pierce
Professional Orchestral
Clarinetist and Instructor

Photo courtesy of David Hall, 1980s.

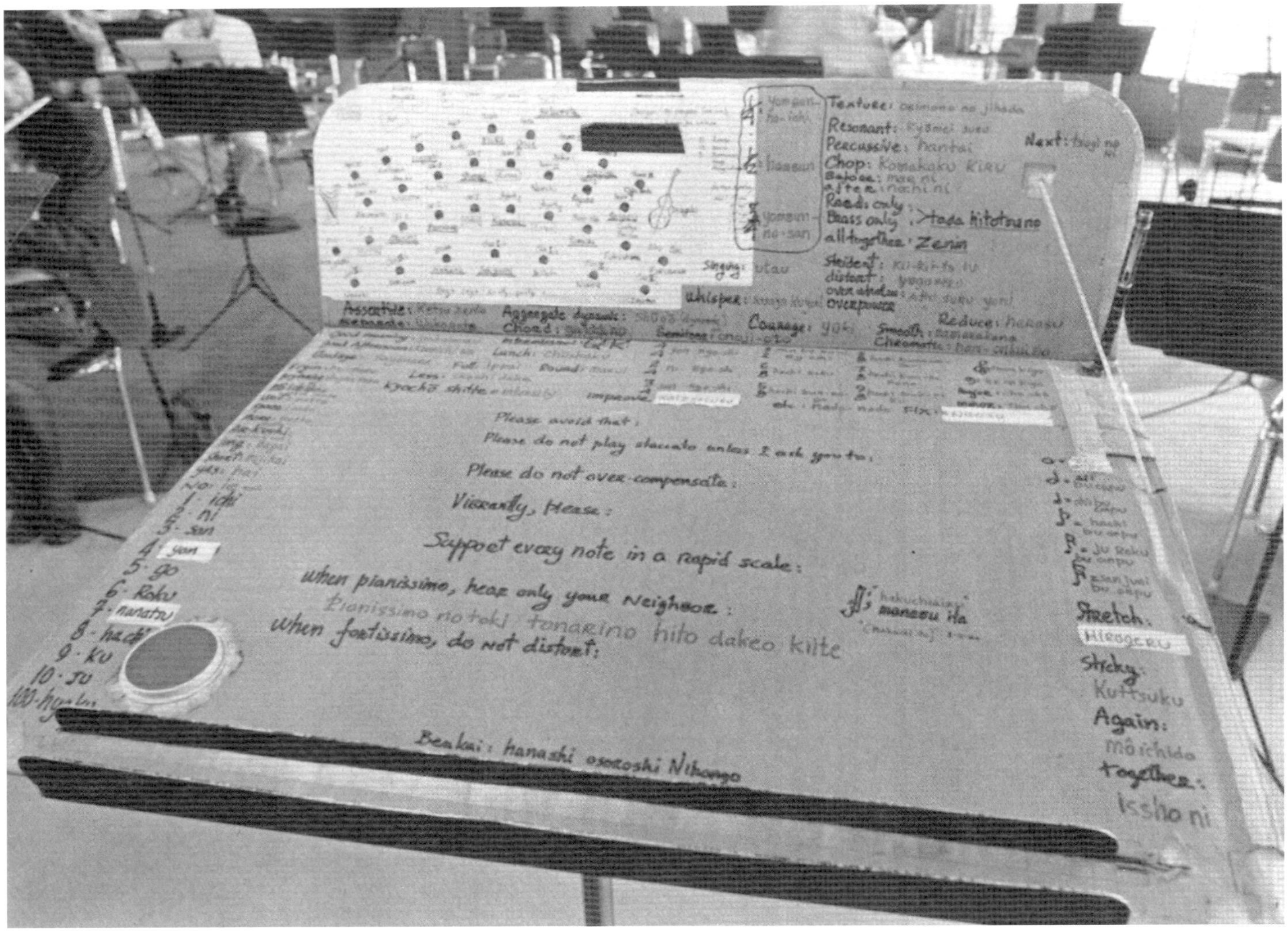

The Maestro called this his "idiot board" including translations of terms and names of the musicians. This was a temporary crutch as he started with Tokyo Kosei Wind Orchestra, 1984.

Mid 1980s, courtesy of Kosei Publishing, photo by Kawamura.

Maestro circa 1984, courtesy of Kosei Publishing, photo by Kawamura.

Vincent Patterson

Fred taught conducting at The Catholic University of America (C.U.) for just one year: 1979. Technically, he had an insatiable appetite for detail in the music no matter what piece we were studying. I'd never seen so many score margin notes, in such miniature, clean penmanship. He also taught me the importance of checking individual parts! This was my first in-depth score/parts study with a conductor who had made musical sense of these works, rehearsed them to his players' understanding, and brought this music to the public's attention successfully. His recipes, and secret ingredients, I still use today.

Of the many "repertoire stories" he freely shared with me, one relates to R. Russell Bennett's *Rag* (*V-Suite of Old American Dances*). Fred chuckled, looking at my clean score, as he said, "They'd call me up about this movement in the middle of the night—the rhythm you know—band directors. Tried to get those rhythms right, they tried and tried." Then he showed me how to do it. What a lesson!

As a Midwestern, fourth-grade saxophone tooter, how could I know one day that guy inside my band folder with the fuzzy crew-cut, bright eyes and "tips" would one day become my teacher, mentor and friend? Hearing about him through the years (until our connection at C.U.) elevated Fred in my mind to HIM status. So, when we met at last, it was Fred's humanness that instantly grabbed me. He didn't swagger, pose, peer nose-long at anyone, or affect his own speech (who in our business hasn't known one of these). "Just do the music," he'd tell me, "and the rest will take care of itself." Whether he's teaching kids how to listen or feeding the koi fish in Tokyo, he is, after all, Fred.

Vincent Patterson
D.M.A.

FF on his 70th birthday. The musicians of the Tokyo Kosei Wind Orchestra all signed this tam-tam as a birthday gift in the Furman Hall Tea Room, July 2, 1984. Photo courtesy of FF.

Gilbert Mitchell

Frederick Fennell and I shared a common love for Percy Grainger and his music. I studied at the Ernest S. Williams School of Music in New York and Percy brought many manuscripts to Williams to play with the band. In fact, they premiered the Grainger *Lincolnshire Posy* (complete) in New York. Again, I played under Percy when he guest conducted in the US Army Band nearly fifty years ago.

In 1988, I sent Fred a tape of my brass choir, Brass of Peace, which included Greig's *Funeral March*. Fred wrote back:

> Things do work in ever-fascinating ways. In your response to one of my suggestions to a committee looking for a really good conductor, you sent a cassette of your Brass of Peace group, and amongst the pieces was Grieg's Nordraak Memorial which I had never heard and knew not at all. It knocked me over!
> Yesterday the Tokyo Kosei Wind Orchestra and I recorded it for Nippon Colu. In an album I'm calling <u>Marches: Satiric – Funeral---Triumphant</u>! I know you can pick the rest of the repertory, too. Jon Eriksen, Chief of Band Music Programs for the Norwegian Broadcast System, set it in B♭ minor for concert band. I've edited it carefully, and my new wife Elizabeth Ludwig Fennell will publish it for the USA & Canada. It is a haunting piece of genuine Grieg, of course, and during its preparation, I kept thinking of two people – you and Percy Grainger. Percy obviously didn't know it anymore than I, but wouldn't he have loved it to pieces. Best, FF

Gilbert Mitchell

In 1983, Lt. Col. Gilbert Mitchell sent FF a recording of Grieg's Funeral March. Mitchell performed this and Lincolnshire Posy *under Percy Grainger at the Ernest S. Williams School of Music in New York. This was the response from FF.*

John R. Beck

In 1992, I was on tour with Keith Brion and the New Sousa Band in Sarasota, Florida. The band heard that Frederick Fennell was in the auditorium, and sure enough at intermission, he appeared backstage. Keith asked him if he would like to conduct one of the marches on the second half of the program. *Kansas Wildcats* was scheduled, and Fennell said that he thought he remembered it. He closed his eyes and began conducting and singing to himself. All the bass drum and cymbal accents were translated to hand, arm, leg, head, and foot gestures. After singing about half of the first strain, he stopped conducting, looked over at Keith and said, "Yes I think I do remember it." As I recall, he didn't use the score for the performance, and the percussion section played with all eyes glued to him.

John R. Beck
Percussionist and Xylophone Soloist
New Sousa Band
Professor of Percussion at the
North Carolina School of the Arts

(FF always believed the number "0" is an important number–constantly overlooked by mathematicians and the general public. "Where would we be without the number 0–we even use it in phone numbers?" That was probably the earful Elizabeth heard on the call Dr. Ginther writes about.)

Dr. John Ginther

Although I have played in adult bands since the 1950s, my career has been as a mathematics professor and therein lies my Fennell anecdote. While I have never met Dr. Fennell in person, I once had the opportunity to speak with him by phone. During a mathematics conference in Cleveland, I visited the Ludwig Music Company, and Mrs. Fennell (its owner) asked me if I'd be interested in speaking, by phone, to Dr. Fennell, who was at their Florida residence. Of course, I eagerly accepted.

Mrs. Fennell dialed FF's number and told him, "Fred, "there's a math teacher here who'd like to talk to you." There was a long silence as she listened to his response, which, of course, I could not hear. Her next comment to him was, "Well don't tell him that or he'll hang up on you!" I'll never know what was said, but apparently the mutual interest that FF and I share in wind music does not extend to mathematics.

I have always enjoyed playing marches, and I consider Dr. Fennell's five-volume set of CDs entitled "*March World-Fennell Best Selection*" to be the finest march recordings of all time. Those CDs are the only ones in my music library for which I have bought back copies, in the event of damage to the main set. Perhaps this is my ultimate compliment to Dr. Fennell's wind-ensemble magic.

Dr. John Ginther
"Professor of Mathematics," University of Michigan

Dennis Beck

When I was growing up in Toronto, my parents had a summer cottage on a lake about ninety minutes north of the city. To avoid heavy weekend traffic, my father would often take an old two-lane highway out of the city. This took us through several small communities, including one which was really just a crossroads consisting of a gas station and a general store. As a teenager, the name of that tiny place, "Fennell's Corners," held no significance for me. Years later, I'd become a band director and passed through that little crossroads, the name of which now meant a great deal to me. I didn't think more of it until several more years had passed, and I had been able to visit and speak with Dr. Fennell at various conferences and workshops. I resolved to take a camera with me the next time I passed through "Fennell's Corners." In the autumn of 1995, I sent an eight by ten of that road sign to Fennell's residence in Florida. About six months later, I received a letter as well as a photo from Dr. Fennell. He was so pleased with the photo that he had framed it and mounted it on the wall of his office at home. He had then taken the time to photograph the new addition to his office so I could see exactly where it hung. His thoughtfulness so inspired me, that I now have the photo and letter he sent back to me hanging in my office. It's something I'll always keep as a personal reminder of the man that has given so much to our profession.

Dennis Beck

Tokyo Kosei Wind Orchestra at Expo Plaza, Tsukubi, July 4, 1985–American Day. The Maestro is on the big screen before performing Copland's Fanfare for the Common Man. Beside the podium is FF's 19th-century rope tension field drum. Photo courtesy of FF.

July 4, 1985. FF has just completed a performance of Connecticut Half-time on his 19th-century rope tension field drum. Photo courtesy of FF.

That spcial look FF has in action. Eyes to the musicians not the music. Circa 1985-86. Photo courtesy of FF by Kawamura.

Max McKee

Fred Fennell: In 1966 Fred Fennell was guest conductor for one of the American Band College Directors' Band concerts in Ashland, Oregon. The event took place at the bandshell in Ashland's beautiful city park. Guest soloists that night were trumpeter Mike Vax and woodwind doubler Gary Foster.

About halfway through the concert, it began to rain. Gary Foster had written out...in ink...a lead for a tune that he and Vax were playing as the rain came down. Within seconds the notes written by Gary literally ran off the page while the rest of us began looking like drowned rats.

Trooper that he is, Fred quickly mounted the podium and ended the concert with a Sousa march. The audience, of course, dispersed almost immediately but Fred and Elizabeth immediately joined the entire band at our home for a post-concert celebration. In my bathrobe with a towel over his head, Fred sat for hours talking with the members of the band and autographing his new book, [the biography]. It was a moment in time that none of us who attended will ever forget.

Max McKee, Director
The American Band College
Southern Oregon University
Ashland, Oregon

Hank Nowak

Maestro Fennell invited me to "come and listen" to his recording session in Yokohama of Moussorgsky's *Pictures at an Exhibition* featuring his famous Japanese wind ensemble. I was Assistant Conductor of the Shanghai Symphony and had called to invite him to its concert in Tokyo. I sat close to the harp and was constantly amazed at the flawless intonation and balance between it and the flutes and tuba. Such an amiable atmosphere of seemingly effortless clarity and precision made me wish I could have witnessed the rehearsals that prepared the ease Fennell displayed on the podium.

Later, as we sat having tea, Maestro Fred, with a wave of his hand referring to his apartment, quipped, "The Diet had to change the national law regarding foreigners to permit me to have this residence in Japan. There is no doubt the Japanese, although wary of foreigners, considered themselves fortunate to have such a man of distinction working among them a few months of the year.

Hank Nowak
Korean National University of Arts
American Ballet Theatre

Photos by Kawamura circa 1986. Courtesy of Kosei Publishing Company.

Photos by Kawamura circa 1986. Courtesy of Kosei Publishing Company.

Photos by Kawamura circa 1986. Courtesy of Kosei Publishing Company.

FF with Jeffrey Renshaw at Eastman. Photo courtesy of Louis Ouzer.

Circa mid 1980s.
Courtesy of Kosei Publishing, photo by Kawamura.

FF on the cover of The Instrumentalist *magazine in October 1986.*
Reprinted with permission from © The Instrumentalist Company.

PERCY ALDRIDGE GRAINGER

Lincolnshire Posy

FULL SCORE EDITION

with newly engraved parts prepared from the autographs by

FREDERICK FENNELL

1. "Lisbon"	1:20
(Sailor's Song)	
2. "Horkstow Grange"	2:40
(The Miser and his Man: A local Tragedy)	
3. "Rufford Park Poachers"	3:35
(Poaching Song)	
4. "The brisk young Sailor"	1:30
(returned to wed his True Love)	
5. "Lord Melbourne"	3:00
(War Song)	
6. "The Lost Lady found"	2:15
(Dance Song)	

With personal best wishes to Rob Simon, one of the conductors Percy Grainger had hoped he would meet through this Really remarkable score.

Frederick Fennell
7 May 1998

Courtesy of Ludwig Music Publishing Company.

1987 Percy Grainger Music Festival at Salem College. Left is Rob Simon, Stewart Manville, curator of the Grainger Society in White Plains, NY, FF and Elizabeth Fennell with pianist Barbara Lister-Sink.

With Vladimir Ussachevsky and Ralph Bigelow, former Registrar of the Eastman School. Photo by Louis Ouzer, circa late 1980s. Portrait of Howard Hanson hangs in the background. Photo courtesy of the Eastman School.

Rehearsal with the EWE.
Photo by Louis Ouzer, 1988, courtesy of the Eastman School.

*Maestro Fennell after receiving an honary doctorate from the University of Rochester.
Photo by Louis Ouzer, 1988, courtesy of the Eastman School.*

WASBE – notes
Jos Frusch

KERKRADE—Have you ever seen a conductor conducting with his back toward the orchestra and facing the concert hall? Me, neither—not until yesterday at 1:30 pm when the wonderful 75-year-old American conductor Frederick Fennell, together with his Tokyo Kosei Wind Orchestra, presented a workshop for conductors in the Wingracht Theater. This fascinating event impressed me especially because it allowed Fennell's public (the conductors participating in the workshop) to be in the position of the orchestra's musicians, this in order to stress what is essential in the art of directing.

In the long run, I will forget much if not all of what happened during this World Music Concours/WASBE Conference, but the figure of that gray-haired conductor will always stay with me: that face, elated at the heavenly sounds of Richard Strauss's *Allerseelen*, those characteristic movements to which his Japanese musicians reacted so accurately, his mimicry and especially that intense radiance.

Conducting the Tokyo Kosei Wind Symphony in the Netherlands, 1989. Photo courtesy of Dries Linssen.

Frederick Fennell clearly showed his eager-to-learn public how a conductor should direct his musicians—with his hands, his eyes, and his entire personality. He began by saying, "I conduct only that which I find important. The architecture of the score determines my movements." He clearly demonstrated what he means by this statement when he showed how it is not to be done-using the music of *Jesu, Joy of Man's Desiring*. As Fennell states, "Communication with the musicians is all important. It is critical to anticipate, to use your eyes and all of your technical faculties."

He then demonstrated this theory with the *Florentiner March* by Fucik. When the first notes from the trumpets sounded just different from and more convincing than we are used to in other renditions, we see a big smile appearing on his face. I have come to see Frederick Fennell as a great artist. He conducts himself like a star.

Translation of review by Jos Frusch accompanied by five candid photographs by Dries Linssen.

Frederick Fennell: "I conduct only that which I find of importance. The architecture of the score determines my movements."

In rehearsal, 1990, courtesy of Kosei Publishing Company, photo by Kawamura.

Shows sense of humor–FF dressed as Bach. Photo courtesy of ELF and Kosei Records.

Cover of *Bandworld* magazine, May 1992. FF and Dr. Earl Slocum, ABA convention, Washington, D.C. Photo courtesy of Max McKee.

Military Bands

Lt. Colonel Philip C. Chevallard

Many years after meeting Frederick Fennell at Interlochen in 1978, I hosted Dr. Fennell in a program I initiated while Commander/Conductor of "America's Band in Blue." The program was a two day affair titled, "Conductor's Day." The first of the two days began with Dr. Fennell rehearsing the musicians and availing them of the history of bands and band music. It was a grand morning and early afternoon for all.

Knowing that Fred shared my interest in trains, I took the rest of the afternoon off and we drove to Old Town Sacramento to see the incredible California Train Museum. He was fascinated by the museum's emphasis on the history of the trans-continental railroad's eastbound component. It was all I could do to tear him away from the steam engine exhibit.

Dr. Fennell spent the entire next day in rehearsals, clinics, and Q & A sessions. Prior to his visit, I asked Fred about his clinician's fee. He responded, "Just pay my expenses; I won't accept a fee—I try to do one military band event every year. This will be the one for 1993. If I had time, I'd certainly do more. It is always a tremendous pleasure to work with America's outstanding professional military bandsmen and bandswomen. It's the least I can do for them."

In my mind, this attitude of service to the arts, teachers, students, and country distinguishes Dr. Fennell as one of America's great leaders and artists. Unequivocally, he has changed and improved music in America and raised public awareness of wind music and bands. He is a man of great integrity and warmth.

Lt. Colonel Philip C. "Carl" Chevallard,
Former Commander/Conductor
The United States Air Force Band of the Rockies

Cmdr. Lewis J. Buckley

All of us in The U.S. Coast Guard Band feel very close to "The Maestro," Frederick Fennell. In addition to all of the other ways in which his life's work has positively affected our world of music-making, he had a very direct impact on our band in May 1981.

The Coast Guard Band invited him to New London, Connecticut to make a guest appearance in our Memorial Day concert. We planned to tape this concert and submit it to National Public Radio in our first attempt at a national broadcast. Not only did we, and our audience, get a great musical experience, but our first NPR broadcast was carried by over eighty stations. This was due entirely to the name and reputation of Frederick Fennell.

We were able to use that first effort as a springboard, and over the next twenty years, we have broadcasted more recorded and live concerts on NPR than any other wind band in America. For beginning what has become one of our most cherished traditions, we will always be grateful to Dr. Fennell.

Cmdr. Lewis J. Buckley
Director, U.S. Coast Guard Band

David Champouillon

As a member of the United States Air Force Band of the Golden Gate from 1979-83, I had the great fortune to play under several premier conductors. During the 1982 Oakland Symphony season, Dr. Fennell was the guest conductor. He planned an all-Sousa program and had numerous local military bandsmen perform with the orchestra to augment the brass section. During the pre-concert warm-up, I happened to pass the Maestro's dressing room. He called me to come in and talk to him while he finished dressing. The memory is forever emblazoned in my mind. Here I am, a twenty-three year-old trumpeter, discussing musical topics with the world famous Frederick Fennell. The fact that made this occasion even more memorable was that he was clad in only in tuxedo shirt, boxer shorts, black knee high socks with garters, and patent leather shoes.

David Champouillon
Department of Music
East Tennessee State University

Colonel Timothy Foley

One of my first acts as director of the Marine Band in 1996 was to invite Fred to conduct a full concert in Baltimore's Meyerhoff Hall. This may not sound unusual, but it marked the first time any "civilian" conducted an entire concert in the Marine Band's two hundred-year history. I also designated Fred as our principal guest conductor, and in that capacity, he returned to conduct our 200th anniversary concert in July 1998.

Of Fred's innumerable qualities, one aspect that makes him unique in our profession is his unbounded joy for music and the totally natural, unaffected way in which he conveys that joy from the podium. I am always amazed by how little he needs to say in rehearsals and by how much comes across in his facial expressions. All of this is not some pre-planned choreography but Fred's perfectly natural response to the music. One look inside Fred's scores reinforces the impression that this man is in love with the music he conducts. His unbelievably meticulous margin notes document a lifetime of observations and experiences. Hearing and seeing Fred conduct is to witness a consummately gifted performer and engaged listener rolled into a truly great conductor.

Colonel Timothy Foley (retired)
"President's Own" Marine Band

Conducting the "President's Own" Marine Band in the Kennedy Center.

*Conducting the "President's Own" Marine Band in the Kennedy Center.
This was the 200th anniversary of the Marine Band, July, 1998.
Photos courtesy of the United States Marine Band and the John F. Kennedy Center for the Performing Arts.*

Elizabeth Ludwig Fennell, Bob Sheldon, Sandy Flesher, and FF at his 80th Birthday Bash, Wickliffe, Ohio, 1994.

Rehearsal with Tokyo Kosei Wind Symphony.
Courtesy of Kosei Publishing, photo by Kawamura.

Leaving his dressing room in Tokyo.
Courtesy of Kosei Publishing, photo by Kawamura, 1995.

Rehearsal with the Tokyo Kosei Wind Orchestra. Courtesy of Kosei Publishing.

Side of stage waiting for entrance.
Courtesy of Kosei Publishing, photo by Kawamura, 1994.

When the Maestro has you in his sights it ensures ultimate precision. Courtesy of Kosei Publishing, photo by Kawamura.

Tuxedo tails on and a warm up before going onstage.
Photo courtesy of Kosei Publishing, photo by Kawamura, 1994.

On stage with the TOKWO, circa mid 1990s.
Courtesy of Kosei Publishing, photo by Kawamura.

FF and his score to Bach Fantasia.
Courtesy of Kosei Publishing, photo by Kawamura.

In rehearsal with TOKWO.
Courtesy of Kosei Publishing, photo by Kawamura, 1995.

Maestro in the office of his apartment in Japan.
Courtesy of Kosei Publishing, photo by Kawamura, 1995.

Reprinted with permission from
Culinary Harmony
"Favorite Recipes of the World's Finest Classical Musicians"
Courtesy of David Rezits, author. Available from DIR Publishers Fort Wayne, IN.

FREDERICK FENNELL, CONDUCTOR

Frederick Fennell is one of the most famous wind ensemble conductors in the world. His numerous recordings, first with the Eastman Wind Ensemble (which he founded in 1952 and has over 30 record releases on the Mercury Living Presence label), and now with the Tokyo Kosei Wind Orchestra (with 25 record releases), are standards against which all other recordings are compared. However, Dr. Fennell is equally at home conducting opera and orchestra. Some of his conducting assignments in these fields are with the Cleveland Orchestra, the London Symphony, and the Denver, New Orleans, St. Louis, National, Buffalo, Houston, Calgary, Eastman, Hartford and San Diego Symphony Orchestras.

Dr. Fennell was an assistant to Serge Koussevitzky at Tanglewood, the assistant music director of the Minneapolis Symphony Orchestra (1962-64), a conducting fellow at the Mozarteum in Salzburg, Austria, and conductor-in-residence at the University of Miami. His opera conducting has included the Eastman Opera Theater and the Houston Light Opera Company. He has conducted the Boston "Pops" Orchestra, the Boston Esplanade and the Carnegie Hall "Pops" Concerts.

Dr. Fennell is editor of *Basic Band Repertory*, *The Instrumentalist* and *BDG*. He has edited many works for wind ensemble that are available through Ludwig Music Publishing Company as well as publications by Fox, Presser and Boosey & Hawkes. A book written about Dr. Fennell by Roger Rickson entitled "FFORTISSIMO" details 40 years of Dr. Fennell's exciting life.

During his most distinguished career, in addition to receiving almost every honor the world can bestow for conducting, he has earned the love and admiration of those who have been fortunate enough to play under his direction and who have come to know him through his appearances all over the world.

The Fennells make their home in Sarasota, Florida, while making frequent trips back to Cleveland to run their Music Publishing Company.

"WHAT'S IN THE FREEZER"?

For my favorite food and its preparation

1. Open the freezer door and select an appropriate item from previous shopping for the evening dinner.

2. Remove from the freezer; follow all instructions from the producer, especially those for piercing the outer plastic sheets with appropriate apertures in the desirable places.

3. Approach the microwave oven.

4. Place the evening's choice within, on micro-acceptable plates, if further garnish on heated plates is your preference.

5. Remove at the sound of the merry 'ting', adding items non-micro, top off with the beverage of choice, according to the foregoing.

Personally, I hate to boil water!

I find this recipe foolproof, inexpensive and frequently very enjoyable. --F.F.

Lifesize cutout of the maestro.

Frederick Fennell Music Camp for conductors was held at Toru Miura's Euphonium Lodge in 2000.

Nichiko Niwano, the president of Rissho-Kosei, presenting Maestro Fennell an award of Special Thanks and announcing FF's appointment as the Laureate Conductor to the TOKWO.

With Toru Miura before a concert.

With Toshio Akiyama who helped arrange FF's appearances in Japan.

Photos courtesy of Kosei Publishing.

Fennell and daughters of Yah Shuhan, the trumpet player from Taiwan.

Photos courtesy of Kosei Publishing.

Maestro always says goodbye to Japanese audiences: Domo Arigato, Sayonara.

Swimming with piccolo/flute player Yasuro Hayasi in a special mainland spot where you can only swim at high tide.

In this picture you can see the famous FF script cufflinks.

He loves Japanese beer!

Fennell talks with TOKWO members with Japanese beer at local restaurant.

Photos courtesy of Kosei Publishing.

Photo courtesy of Loras John Schissel.

*Frederick Fennell Concert Hall in Kafu, Japan.
Photo courtesy of FF.*

Ronald Broun

The legendary Frederick Fennell—the greatest conductor of wind ensembles or, if you prefer, music for band—is, at eighty-seven, so full of sap you wouldn't believe it. This is the man who, in the 1950s, astonished the world (and this reviewer) with his Mercury recordings by the Eastman Symphonic Wind Ensemble. That achievement set a standard for band music that has never been equaled, except by Fennell himself.

Thirteen original members of Fennell's Eastman Ensemble were on hand to honor him Saturday afternoon at the Library of Congress's Coolidge Auditorium. They joined twenty-three musicians to form a wind ensemble led by Fennell. The ensemble performed works by Grainger, Persichetti, Hartley, Piston, Bennett and Sousa.

Fennell had lost nothing to age. As always, he was sensational. Demonstrating on a nineteenth-century rope-tension field drum, Fennell explained with a wolfish grin how music for fife and drums should go and then rapped it out with startling energy and precision. His Sousa marches—*Fairest of the Fair*, *Black Horse Troop* and *King Cotton*—were nonpareil. Piston's *Tunbridge Fair*, a tartly ragged, multi-voiced commemoration of a Vermont fair, surely never sounded so good. Hartley's *Concerto for 23 Winds* was lithe and supple and everything else on the program sounded sweet, robust, and…well, like Frederick Fennell was conducting.

Ronald Broun
Washington Post Music Review
May 20, 2001

Elizabeth and Fred, 2001, after the Library of Congress concert, Washington, D.C. Photo courtesy of Robert Simon.

2001, FF being inducted to the Classic Music Hall of Fame. The evening was for Fred and Van Cliburn. Photo courtesy of Dorothy Kemp.

Fred with his 19th-century rope tension field drum on the stage in Coolidge Auditorium. Photo by Robert Simon, 2001.

Chris Donze

It was the evening of November 16, 2003 when we finished recording *You've Been Verrry Good* with the Frederick Fennell Symphonic Winds in Indianapolis Indiana. Many of the musicians had already taken a cab to the airport or begun a satisfied ride home. The only people left to dine together were Fred, his wife, Elizabeth Ludwig-Fennell, composer and percussionist Clarence Barber, and I. As we soaked up the afterglow of several days' successful work, we talked about the future of band music in America.

When the conversation drew to a momentary lull, the look in Fred's eye changed as he gathered in the silence, preparing to speak: "Are you familiar with the subway booth that rises up from the sidewalk on Michigan Avenue in Chicago, near Congress Hotel?" For anyone who frequents the Midwest Band and Orchestra Clinic, the spot Fred described is on the route from Congress Hotel to the Hilton. Fred continued, "One year at the Midwest Clinic, while I was walking past that point, a man came up from the stairwell and approached me. He looked to be in his late sixties and possibly homeless; he wore a tattered coat with patched elbows, a worn knit hat, and torn, fingerless gloves. He seemed very content as he drew near. 'Excuse me, sir. Are you Frederick Fennell?' the man asked with some excitement. He seemed thrilled to have found me when I responded in the affirmative.

Fred held all of our attention as he continued relating what the strange man had said to him: "'I have something in my coat pocket for you, and you may have it if you agree to several conditions that I will explain. It can only be used toward the accomplishment of one goal, but you may decide how best to achieve that goal. Are you interested? It is a check for fifty million dollars.'" I stopped swallowing my food as I was stunned by the idea. What happened to the check? What were the conditions? My mind raced, but I remained quiet as Fred saw all of those thoughts running across my puzzled face. He continued, "I was instructed to use the money to establish a new professional music performance group—a band. I was to hire only the best professionals to play in the band, and I was to be the conductor. There was one other catch." I waited as Fred obviously savored the coming line: "All performances were to take place on the same nights that the Chicago Symphony performed. The audience would have to choose who they would listen to for every performance."

With a impish grin and quick nod, Fred confirmed what we knew was likely to happen in such a case. The audience was almost certain to choose a band performance over that of a symphony, even one as outstanding as the Chicago Symphony. I had to ask, "Did you really meet this guy?" "Not yet," replied Fred with a wink, "but each year I go to the Midwest, I dream that maybe this year we will meet."

It occurred to me over the next several days that Fred was not so much teasing us as he was sharing with us his dream. I felt as if he was assigning me a task. Fred wanted me to carry the anticipation and be ready for the moment when a new age of concert bands would begin, the age in which concerts halls would be full of appreciative audiences clamoring for the band. It worked. I believe in that day and am willingly preparing for its arrival.

Chris Donze
President of Ludwig Music Publishing

Cover of Bandworld *magazine, March 2003. Ray E. Cramer congratulates his good friend, FF, during the Tokyo Kosei Wind Orchestra concert during the 56th annual Midwest Band Clinic. Photo by Jonathan Kim, courtesy of Max McKee.*

Jerry Junkin

Frederick Fennell is, and has been, a national treasure. The godfather of the modern wind band has enjoyed a warm relationship for nearly twenty years with the musicians and concert-going public of the city of Dallas. From his first appearance with the Dallas Wind Symphony, he has been one of the true champions of the band and has helped put us on the map through his recordings, concerts and special appearances.

He was a great friend and advisor to Howard Dunn, the founding conductor of the Dallas Wind Symphony, and continues to provide sage advice to both executive director Kim Campbell and myself. He is inspiring in every way, and all of us with the Dallas Wind Symphony are indebted to him, not only for his efforts on our behalf, but for his staggering contributions to our profession.

Jerry Junkin
Artistic Director and Conductor
Dallas Wind Symphony

FF and Jerry Junkin of the Dallas Wind Symphony. Photo courtesy of Kevin Reed, 1998.

FF conducting Dallas Wind Symphony, photo courtesy of Kevin Reed.

With Dallas Wind Symphony, courtesy of Kevin Reed.

Additional photographs in Dallas by Kevin Reed.

The FF excitement in rehearsal with the Dallas Wind Symphony, photos courtesy of Kevin Reed.

Additional photographs in Dallas by Kevin Reed.

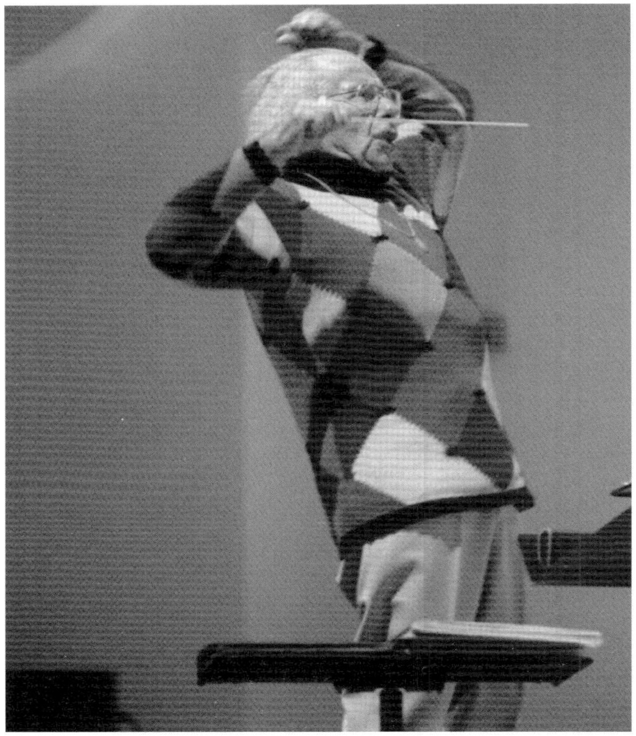

Exuberance captured on the podium in a rehearsal with the Piedmont Wind Symphony at Wake Forest University in Winston-Salem, NC.

FF in concert with the Piedmont Wind Symphony at Wake Forest University in Winston-Salem, NC, 1998.

FF in concert with the Piedmont Wind Symphony at Wake Forest University in Winston-Salem, NC, 1998.

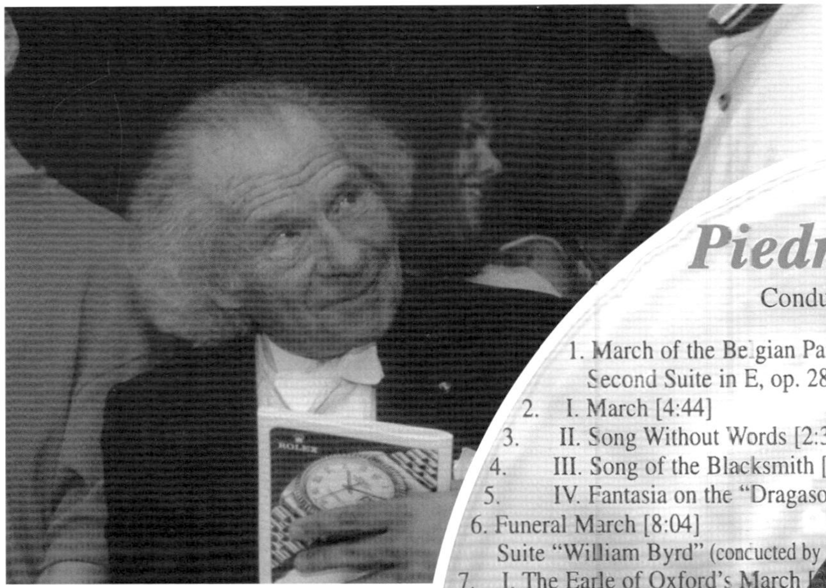

PIEDMONT WIND SYMPHONY

www.piedmontwindsymphony.com

336.722.9328

FF conducts the PWS in a performance of Lover Man, *featuring Patrick Tucker on flugelhorn.*

FF in discussion with PWS principal players Linda Julian (clarinet) and Jonathan Julian (bassoon).

At an Eastman reunion with former faculty, Emily Vanderpool and Gladys Leveton, 1996. Photo courtesy of the Eastman School.

75th Anniversary Season
2000–2001

Best Wishes
Concerts from the Library of Congress
to
the Music Division
from
The William and Flora Hewlett Foundation
Frederick Fennell

FREDERICK FENNELL CONDUCTS
MUSIC FOR WIND ENSEMBLE

Saturday, May 19, 2001
2 o'clock in the afternoon
Coolidge Auditorium
Thomas Jefferson Building

Washington, DC, 2001.
Photo courtesy by Joan Templar Smith.

Following the May 19 Wind Band Concert at the Library of Congress, a moment of camaraderie is shared by (front row) Frederick Fennell, oboist Sandra Flesher, bassoonist Phillip Kolker, Rosemary Crawford Fetter, trombonist David Fetter, and (visible in back) contrabassist Elizabeth Twaddell Ferrell, bassonist Eric Dirkson, and French hornist Carl Bianchi. Washington, DC, 2001. →

In Washington, DC, with Robert (Bob) Sheldon, 2001.

*FF's hands over copies of his Library of Congress publication on the analysis of Sousa's Stars and Stripes Forever.
Photo courtesy of Robert Sheldon.*

Celebrating Fennell at 90
An Appreciation by Loras John Schissel

The most vivid and touching memory I have of this remarkable musician dates from a few years ago. The Library of Congress had engaged Fennell to conduct a wind ensemble concert in our historic Coolidge Auditorium. The musicians, selected by Robert Sheldon, an Eastman Wind Ensemble alumnus, and the curator of the musical instruments collections at the Library, were primarily former Eastman alumni and Fennell's students. To my great delight, Sheldon asked me to play euphonium in the ensemble.

The concert was everything one would expect with Fennell on the podium and fine musicians playing...but it was seeing and experiencing the almost child-like delight these seasoned (and somewhat grizled) musicians took in being with and more importantly making music with this great man. "Those Eastman Kids" he calls them, scattered throughout the world now. In a way they really are his kids. Such a special time, those wonderous years in the fifties and early sixties at Eastman, and how Fennell "his kids" changed the face of wind-band music.

The recordings have taught me more music than a whole wall of degrees possibly could. I can say without a doubt, that Frederick Fennell is one of the most important wind-band musicians...ever. The recordings document the music for the future, but it's the lives he has touched, the countless young musicians he's encouraged, the quest for excellence which he has inspired that is Fennell's legacy. For him, it's all about the music...it's all about "those kids." You've been the guiding spirit in my life, something I can always count on. God bless you, Fred. Happy 90th, and most importantly... Thank you!

Loras John Schissel

Presenting FF the cover to his book during rehearsal in Severance Hall on Fred's 90th birthday. Loras John Schissel, FF and Rob Simon. Photo by Roger Mastroianni, courtesy of the Cleveland Orchestra. July 2, 2004.

Rehearsal, Summer 2004 in Severance Hall. Photos courtesy of Roger Mastrorianni and the Cleveland Orchestra.

Over 14,000 fans attend the concert at the Blossom Music Center and sing "Happy Birthday" to the Maestro for his 90th. The band includes wind players of the Cleveland Orchestra. Blossom is situated on 800 acres of rolling hills surrounded by the Cuyahoga River. Photos by Roger Mastroianni, courtesy of the Cleveland Orchestra, 2004.

Blossom Music Center

FF, Loras John Schissel and the Blossom Band of the Cleveland Orchestra celebrate the Maestro's 90th birthday.

The 1952
Yaddo Music Group
presents

SIX CONCERTS
of
CONTEMPORARY AMERICAN
MUSIC

In Observance of Yaddo's First Twenty-five
Years of Service to the Arts

SEPTEMBER 12th, 13th and 14th

at

Yaddo

Saratoga Springs, New York

Sponsored by The Corporation of Yaddo

KEEP THIS PROGRAM FOR ALL CONCERTS

Please do not smoke in the Music Room

Fourth Concert

Saturday evening at eight

The Yaddo Orchestra
Frederick Fennell, conductor

WALTER PISTON — Divertimento (1946)
    allegro
    tranquillo
    vivo

HOWARD HANSON — Pastorale for Oboe and Strings (1949)
    andante piacevole
    Robert Lehrfeld, oboe

CHARLES IVES — Symphony III (1911)
    andante maestoso
    allegro
    largo

— INTERMISSION —

SAMUEL BARBER — Capricorn Concerto (1945)
    allegro ma non troppo
    allegretto
    allegro con brio
    Albert Saurini, flute
    Robert Zupnik, oboe
    Thomas Hohstadt, trumpet

HOWARD BOATWRIGHT — Variations for Small Orchestra (1949)
    Theme - fast
    variations 1   very slow
                2   gigue - moderately fast
                3   fanfare - somewhat faster
                4   trio - scherzando
                5   nocturne - moderately slow
                6   march - vigorous
    fugue - moderately flowing

WALTER HARTLEY — Triptych (1952)
    adagio
    allegro con fuoco
    andante sostenuto ma con moto

Program from Yaddo Music Group, 1952.

ROCHESTER TIMES-UNION
Mon., Sept. 15, 1952 — 15

Yaddo Fest Offers Rich Music Treat

By ADELE M. WOODWORTH
Music critic of The Saratogian

Saratoga Springs — Orchestral music of high order, both from the standpoint of composer and performance, was heard this weekend at Yaddo, famed music and art center here in this New York State resort town.

A feature of the festival, an annual event that draws many of the nation's top musicians and young composers to the huge elm-shaded estate now devoted to the arts, was Saturday night's concert by the Yaddo Festival Orchestra conducted by Frederick Fennell, associate conductor of Eastman School of Music orchestras and band. This drew the largest audience of the weekend and won for composers represented, the conductor and the orchestra repeated rounds of appreciative applause from an unusually large audience.

Rochester's Eastman School was well represented in the membership of the orchestra, more than half of the personnel of the 30-piece little symphony having been associated in study or other musical capacity with the school. A composition by its director, Dr. Howard Hanson, was included in Saturday night's concert.

• • •

FIRST OFFERING of the evening was Walter Piston's Divertimento. Under Fennell's capable and enthusiastic direction, the three movements of this work drew for its sustained high register virile bowing from the string section and clear smooth tones in the other instruments.

The Hanson number was exceptionally well performed, providing one of the highlights of the program. This Pastorale for Oboe and Strings is all sheen and sheer beauty. It reflects a surging motif which rises to the heights then ebbs while through it flows the fluid, clear oboe melody. The Pastorale was given an excellent playing with special kudos for Robert Lehrfeld, oboe soloist.

Charles Ives' Symphony No. 3, written in 1911, which found itself congenial with the more modern constituents who abound at these annual conclaves, and Samuel Barber's Capricorn Concerto followed on the program. Albert Saurini, flute; Robert Zupnik, oboe, and Thomas Hohstadt, trumpet, were soloists in the latter selection.

• • •

Fennell Letters

Hillhouse West Mill Road
Philadelphia 28, Pa.
March 1, 1953

Dear Mr. Fennell

    I was delighted with your performance of my Divertimento last Monday. The Ensemble is a brilliant and supple one – your line and phrase shapes were distinguished.

    Mr. Langenus of Presser Co. has written me regarding the possibility of your recording the entire work for Mercury Records. Your performance is the one I like best so naturally I would be happy to have you record it.

Sincerely,

Vincent Persichetti

Letter from Vincent Persichetti to Frederick Fennell from the archive in the Sibley Library at the Eastman School of Music.

TIME AND THE WINDS

A Short History of The Use of Wind Instruments in The Orchestra, Band and The Wind Ensemble

by
FREDERICK FENNELL

Dear Rose,
I wrote this little book in a white-hot heat – two months in the summer of 1953. The few notes about the alto clarinet are all that was changed from my ms.

Frederick Fennell
5 oct 03

LeBlanc Publication by Frederick written in 1953 is still a standard today.

Nov. 10, 1956

From
Percy Grainger
7 Cromwell Place
White Plains, N.Y.

Dear Frederick (Fennell)

Just back from concerts in Iowa & New Mexico. I find your lovely letter of Nov 8, with its wonderful news that you are doing the *Posy* next Friday. **How wonderful for me!** Of course I would **love** to have a tape of your performance. I am so elated that you **like** the score of the *Posy*.

Because of my concerts I postponed answering your long letter (Oct 11), the contents of which thrilled me beyond words. I had no idea that my band music & my attitude to the band had meant anything to you so long ago. There is no honor comparable to the fact of you approving of my band music, because no one in the band field can compare with you ---- in rightness of sonorities, in subtlety, in refinement, in drastic & fearless mastery, in brilliance, in expressiveness.

You write of 4 scores of both *Hillsongs*. Does that mean that I sent you the score of *Hillsong I*? I didn't think I had one. But I have now heard that perhaps I can get a score of *Hillsong 1* from Universal Edition, Vienna. **But is it any use to you, with its strings, piano & harmonium?** Even if it is **no use** to you I will be happy to give you the score (if I can get it) as a token of our tone-fellowship-- if you would care to have it.

In the meantime, I cannot tell you how elated I am at your doing **Posy**.

Love from us both,
Percy

THE UNIVERSITY OF ROCHESTER
Eastman School of Music

January 30, 1957

Mr. Percy Grainger
7 Cromwell Place
White Plains, New York

Dear Percy:

I fear that this letter will not have reached you before you have left the country, but I shall send it on in any case for I am always so happy to have letters from you.

They are filled with the enthusiasm of a man who is neither young nor old, but truly alive. They always give me great stimulation in the same way that your music has always given me great feeling of warmth and true musical joy.

I can only say that I am desperately trying to find funds to expand our recording program which is to include at the earliest possible time recording of the **POSY** and the **Hillsong N0. 2.**

With warmest regards to you and your Princess, I am

Cordially yours,
Frederick Fennell,
Conductor

THE UNIVERSITY OF ROCHESTER
EASTMAN SCHOOL OF MUSIC

June 28, 1957

Mr. Percy Grainger
7 Cromwell Place
White Plains, New York

Dear Percy:

I am so happy to have your two letters of recent date and to know that you are back in the country. It is disturbing to know that you have been under the need of medical care and I sincerely hope that this is nothing serious.

I am so happy to tell you, Percy, that when we are able to record the **LINCOLNSHIRE POSY** and any other music of yours, that it will not only not demand any funds from you for us to do so, but that it is intended that out of your ASCAP royalties and your general composer royalties that you should indeed receive such benefits as sales of the record would make possible. I know so well that all of your life you have undertaken publication of your own things also I am sure at great expense. I also know that you have never been the slightest bit hesitant to assist anybody who was interested. Knowing that this has been your necessary pattern in the past. I am so happy to say that we do not expect any financial help from you. It is my fervent hope that we shall be able to record the **LINCOLNSHIRE POSY** this winter. As soon as dates ad everything else are settled, I will most certainly let you know. Most of all, I am happy that you did get back into the country safely.

With all good wishes to you and Mrs. Grainger, I am

Cordially yours,

Frederick Fennell
Conductor

p.s. Thanks for the so beautiful Stockholm card and the nice words about my Anderson record. FF

Reprinted are letters between FF and Percy Grainger, courtesy of the Library of Congress

Covers of the reissues of earlier Mercury recordings
Courtesy of Universal Polygram

THE UNIVERSITY OF ROCHESTER
EASTMAN SCHOOL OF MUSIC
ROCHESTER 4, NEW YORK

April 8, 1958

Mr. Percy Grainger
7 Cromwell Place
White Plains, New York

Dear Percy:

By now we trust you have returned home from your arduous journeys about the country. I tried to contact you at Waco at recording time and they could only give me Saginaw as forwarding so I missed you. The POSY is safely recorded for posterity and its judgements. You did your part so magnificently that we can only hope that our final results will be worthy of yours. It is recorded in our single microphone (telefunken) technique for the monaural LP and in three-channel stereophonic sound (three telefunkens on Ampex recorder). In all of my eleven previous LP's I never had quite as much difficulty getting exactly what I wanted. The POSY took me an unbelievable sixty-three minutes to record! Such a transparent score — such a very trickly piece of music to record — and we all were trying so hard to get it exactly as we wanted it. No piece or group of pieces ever took so much time and please don't be disturbed by this. The engineer and the recording directors were as fussy as I was since I had fully primed them on its importance and my love for it.

Now as soon as the stereophonic tape is edited according to my preferred takes, I want you and the Princess to plan to come to New York City at the Mercury offices to hear it. I don't expect that editing will be completed before May 1st even though the recording took place on March 2nd. Things are so busy with Mercury that it will take some time before the editing of a winter's recording will keep pace with test pressings.

I heard all the takes before Mercury left here and I was as satisfied as I ever am with what I did and that does not mean that I am proud of myself. I am **very** proud of my players, however, who did a fantastic job of playing it.

Coupling on the album will be you and the Strauss Eb SERENADE for one side and Milhaud's SUITE FRANCAISE and Bernard Rogers' JAPANESE DANCES for the reverse. A really wonderful record and one which nobody but I would make and Mercury would be willing to record. The next day I did another album of all the rest of Leroy Anderson's charming little pieces with my orchestra, and later that evening the Wind Ensemble recorded the 10TH SERENADE IN Bb by Mozart, that simply glorious pean of sound for thirteen winds. I waited to live long enough to make this record. We got it in an incredibly short 3 1/2 hours for a 44 minute work, used basset horns of course and string bass, contrabassoon, and contrabass clarinet for the bottom. I am most anxious to have you hear this too.

I am working on the liner notes for the album and trust that I may quote from your foreward to the score. Too bad I can't print it all. Your performance with Dick Goldman and the Band is very good indeed, and how wonderful it is

Mr. Percy Grainger
Page Two
April 9, 1958

that some of these things will be available to those who have ears to hear! I wrote David Hall about our recording the POSY and I have suggested that he ask you to write an article for his new magazine, HI FI AND MUSIC REVIEW on you and winds and how come you believed when almost nobody and how you fit into my own formation of the Wind Ensemble. I do hope he will ask you to do it in connection with the album's release scheduled for Fall. Thanks so much for the beautiful POSY. I'll be in touch with you about coming to Mercury in New York.

Love,

Frederick Fennell,
Conductor

Letter from FF to Grainger about the recording of Lincolnshire Posy.
Courtesy of the Library of Congress.

Dear Graingers:

Today Wilma Cozart, V.P. of Mercury called to ask what I would think of my doing an all Grainger recording with The Eastman-Rochester Pops Orchestra! Of course I jumped at the chance. What they want has been triggered by the Posy which they all simply love. They want Molly, Spoon, Irish Tune, Gardens – anything that I want to do. So, do sit thee doon and let me have your ideas of what my Grainger album should contain.

I have the perfect cover photo for the album, one of those I took of you last September. It's my Best portrait in color. How nice of you to write your reactions to the Mozart, and illuminating reactions they are. Indeed the basset has a flute quality.

Happy New Year to you both - Love
ff

What a wonderful New Year - January 1959

Photo courtesy of Universal Polygram Records

Letter from FF to Grainger, New Years, 1959, about the request of Mercury to record an all-Grainger album. Courtesy of the Library of Congress.

Jan 5, 1959 7 Cromwell Place, White Plains, N.Y.

Dear Frederick,

Thanks for your dear letter of Jan 4 with its good wishes for 1959, but there is no need for good wishes (one is tempted to say) when the good luck has already happened. I refer to Mercury's suggestion that you do an All-Grainger album. This is QUITE UNBELIEVABLE, isnt it? As you say, it all goes back to your superb recording of the POSY. As Wagner makes Hans Sachs say in Meistersinger: Wer hätt's gedacht, was doch recht Wort und Vortrag macht! (Who would have believed what the right words & the right expression can accomplish) So I must send you a new salvo of thanks for the unbelievable you already have done, & a 2nd salvo for what you intend to do.

We are so delighted that your color photo of me came out so well & that we shall have the pleasure of seeing it on the album cover.

As to my ideas for the contents of the album, my first thought is that we must not burden Mercury with too many "unpopular" pieces seeing that they already have recorded a long & somewhat hard-to-take piece in the POSY. Of course we should include all the numbers the V.P. mentioned (Molly, Spoon, Irish Tune, Country Gardens) & perhaps you should consider HANDEL IN THE STRAND & Mock Morris as well--among the already-known ones. Also COLONIAL SONG (not using the 2 voices) which plays about 6 minutes, & EARLY ONE MORNING, which plays about 5 minutes. these last-mentioned 2 pieces, being gentle & melodious, would provide contrast to the livelier things.

Would it mean filling both sides of a long-playing disc? If so, I suppose we might have to consider a longer work of not too dance-like a character. The works I would love to hear someday from incomparable baton are the following, in the order of their importance to me:

Hill-Song I, chamber orchestra, about 14 minutes
ENGLISH DANCE, orchestra & organ, about 8 minutes
HILL-SONG II, orchestra without trombones, tuba, violins (violas & cellos substitute for the 4 saxs) 4 1/2
THE WARRIORS, orchestra, tuneful percussion & 3 pianos, 18 minutes.

Altho the above longer & less popular pieces are close to my heart, I do not recommend them for the album. If a longer work seems desirable I would recommend SUITE "IN A NUTSHELL" for orchestra, piano & tuneful percussion, about 18 minutes. I would (if desired) play the piano part, without fee, & Ella (if desired) would play some of the more unusual tuneful percussion (staff bells, wooden marimba, vibraharp) as she also would in THE WARRIORS. But in both these works (Warriors & NUTSHELL) other percussion players would be needed, in addition to Ella": 1 player on glock., 1 on xylophone, one or 2 on vibraharp, one or 2 on wooden marimba. It is scandalous how the more delicate-toned percussion have been ignored while the harsh-toned ones (xylo. & glock.). "Tho I says it as shouldnt" the work I have done with the gentler percussion is worthy of attention & the combined sonorities of these gentler instruments would be wonderful on records. If you decided on any work using the extra percussion I would come to Rochester well in advance (if you could gather for me some pianists or other musical percussionists) & train them in the pipes, get them to use the right mallets (most important).

I am sending you the score of my ENGLISH WALTZ, which has never been recorded & is, I think, a good number. I will supply any of the numbers you dont have, & I will play the piano part in any numbers (if you would like it) that call for a more or less prominent piano part ("yes" in NUTSHELL, "no" in ENGLISH DANCE, for instance. Please dont let the contents of this letter lead us into a high brow choice of program that nobody but you & I would enjoy. Mercury has been so good to me & if an album of my things be decided upon, let it be a rewarding album for Mercury. Please forgive this hasty & ill-considered letter. I wanted to get a happy & thankfull reply to you quickly.   Yours gratefully

Percy Grainger

Jan 6, 1959 7 Cromwell Place, White Plains, N.Y.

Dear Frederick,

I am sorry that the letter I wrote you yesterday was so feeble in so many ways. The main feebleness stems from the chronology of my composing. If folksong had been my first love & I had turned to polyphonic & symphonic music later on (what is called "development") I would not think it unnatural that people consider folktunes & other bits of small form to be my natural medium & consider pieces such as ENGLISH DANCE & HILL-SONG as something I had acquired later & which did not fit me so well. I would consider such an opinion reasonable because I believe that the best years for composing are the years of "juvenile delinquency". But what actually happened with me as a composer was just the opposite of that. It was Bach's long-flow form that I fell in love with around the age of 10, whereas folksong did not reach me at all until the age of about 18 & seriously only at the age of 22. So I had more than 10 years between discovering Bach at the age of 10 & discovering folksongs, & in those years I had every opportunity (& made the most of them) to fall in love with the "long flow" of Wagner, Brahms, Cyril Scott. Of all the music that I heard in Germany the first chorus of Bach's Mathew Passion was the most satisfying & even today it is still my favorite piece of music--such glorious lengths, such a lovely muddle. (Compared to it the Prelude to Tristan is intermittant & piecemeal-y) So out of this first-chorus-in-the-Mathew-Passion background things like the Hillsongs, Bushmusic, Sea-music, English Dance, Train-Music were born. And since these things were my first musical love it is only natural that I like hearing them played & would like to see them recorded some day--MOST ESPECIALLY by you.

But that doesnt mean that I expect the general public (or even the normal musicians) to share my taste. If they saw eye to eye with me they would worship the 1st chorus of the Mathew Passion as I do. But as they dont, why should we expect them to like compositions which are derived from the 1st chorus? (There are many good musicians who prefer the last chorus to the 1st chorus.) And why not? Perhaps they like melody more than I do. I am not against melody, but I evidently do not like it enough to be able to write GOOD melody.

So it is probably true that my lack of good melody outlaws my larger works with the general public. On the other hand, I think it may be said that the public likes my choice of melody--melody written by others. And the public may even (in a blind sort of way) somewhat like the Bach-derived rich polyphonic & harmonic sauce that I pour over other people's tunes.

Of course, I was no disliker of melody. One reason why I threw myself over folksong was that I wanted to study the nature of good melody in the hopes of one day being able to write it myself. But this hope was never realised. The music I can claim is to be able, sometimes, to write good counter-melodies, such as those in GREENBUSHES. By the way, GREEN BUSHES is my best orchestral folkmusic setting. Do you know it? If not, shall I send it to you?

What is one to say of my IMITATIONS of melody--in MOCK MORRIS, HANDEL IN THE STRAND, COLONIAL SONG--does the public take to them as to genuine melody, or does it sense something 2nd hand? That is a question not yet decided perhaps. Years ago HANDEL IN THE STRAND could not compete with my folksong settings. Today I think it is on a par with them. And COLONIAL SONG seems to me to have made many friends. By the way, I have had to revise its end. So if you choose it for the album I must let you have a corrected score & parts.

Have you any idea when you might be doing the album? Because we are planning to go to Europe in April or May. But if you would like me to play the piano in any numbers we might alter our sailing date so as to be here when you want me if you do want me.

Why I mentioned SUITE "IN A NUTSHELL" as a possible longer work is because it is melodically not too weak. The final march is pleasing, the slow movement is my best slow movement for orchestra, "Gay but wistful" is much liked, the first movement is perhaps unique in that it is unharmonised.

Letters from Grainger to FF about recording repetory from January 5 and 6, 1959. Courtesy of the Library of Congress.

THE UNIVERSITY OF ROCHESTER
EASTMAN SCHOOL OF MUSIC
ROCHESTER 4, NEW YORK

April 17, 1959

Mr. Percy Grainger
7 Cromwell Place
White Plains, New York

Dear Percy:

This is the final plan on your record: Two sides of the following pieces: COUNTRY GARDENS, HANDEL, MOCK, IRISH TUNE, MOLLY, SPOON, CHILDREN'S MARCH, ROBIN IS TO THE GREENWOOD, SHEPHERDS, IMMOVABLE DO, COLONIAL SONG.

Can you send me before you go a set of parts to EARLY ONE MORNING in case we need that too? Strings 5-4-3-2-2.

I am so happy to tell you also that we are recording HILL SONG NO. 2 with the Wind Ensemble on Monday, May 4th. This is the big Grainger push and I am so honored at this chance to do what little I can to preserve your great music by making it possible for the deaf to hear it and the blind to see the scores.

If that happens for any of your things as a result of these records, then I will have done at least one good thing in my life.

You must send me your addresses while abroad. I'll be writing again before you sail. Send exact date and time of sailing.

Affectionately,

Frederick Fennell,
Conductor

FF:mz

Letter from FF to Grainger about the recording of Hill Song No. 2 and eleven other orchestral pieces.

WESTERN UNION TELEGRAM

SYA160

SY RHA263 PD ROCHESTR NY 1 947AME 1959 MAY 1 AM 10 36

PERCY GRAINGER=

7 CROMWELL PL WHITE PLAINS NY.

B FLAT CONTRABASS CLARINET WRITTEN AS REGULAR BASS CLARINET IN TREBLE CLEFF BUT SOUNDS ONE OCTAVE LOWER WILL USE CONTRA PART IF ARRIVE BEFORE MONDAY MORNING THINGS IN GOOD SHAPE FOR YOUR SESSION SORRY YOU CANT BE WITH US AFFECTIONATELY=

FREDERICK FENNELL EASTMAN SCHOOL OF MUSIC=

150 Commodore Parkway
Rochester, N.Y.

Great Marches are Forever!
Frederick Fennell

Photo of FF listening to a march from his five volume series of marches in the Brain Recordings. Courtesy of Brain Co., Ltd., Hiroshima, Japan.

THE UNIVERSITY OF ROCHESTER
EASTMAN SCHOOL OF MUSIC
ROCHESTER 4, NEW YORK

May 20, 1959

Mr. Percy A. Grainger
c/o Mrs. R.C. Bristow
Southolm, Pevensy Bay
Sussex, ENGLAND

Dear Percy:

We got <u>fine</u> recordings of the eleven orchestral pieces and HILL SONG NO. 2. We did the orchestral things on Sunday night (for 3 1/2 hours) and on Tuesday morning, May 3 & 5. We interspersed ten other pieces of standard encore fare in between your titles to break up the routine to everybody's advantage. Those ten pieces will come out as an album of "chestnuts" and your eleven titles will be an album all by themselves.

Of all of your beautiful and enchanting things we did for orchestra the one which has taken me over the deepest is COLONIAL SONG, and how <u>grateful</u> I am that you sent me your Schott edition in E major! That G. Schirmer E flat version is not quite the same piece and I think you will be warmed by our performance of this most lovely original work of yours in the revised set you sent. All of your things are treacherous to play well -- HEY is devilish -- MOLLY is a string player's downfall if he thinks it's easy (and a conductor's, too!). We got a good balance on all the percussion and piano and organ in those tunes that called for same. I remember playing SPOON RIVER with you in Cleveland's Public Auditorium in April 1932 when I was a steel marimba player in the National High School Orchestra and you conducted a massive piano ensemble. I vividly remember seeing you go along that row of grands, raising each lid -- your beautiful cape flying from your shoulders. I thought of this during the recording session.

We cannot expect to hear a test any sooner than from ten months to a year. They are so swamped with releases and so much editing is required for stereo and monaural that they only edit each tape as a particular album comes close to that time (scheduled far in advance) for its release. For instance, our album of International Marches, HANDS ACROSS THE SEA, was recorded last November 6th and my test tape only came last week -- five month later. The Volume II of BRITISH BAND CLASSICS will not be released until September and I don't expect a test on that until August.

The HILLSONG was such a joy to do and I hope you will like our performance. We used the large ensemble version with the advantages the low brass give to those crucial punctuation points throughout. The Selmer people sent us a beautiful soprano sax for it, too.

All together, Percy, it was quite a three days of recording for me with four sessions in that time. We started out with a four-hour session on Sunday morning the 3rd from 9:00 to 1:00, recording in that time Morton Gould's WEST POINT SYMPHONY, Clifton Williams' FANFARE AND ALLEGRO, Julian Work's AUTUMN WALK, and Russell Bennett's SYMPHONIC SONGS. Then after a few hours of rest they set up my orchestra and I recorded you and Rimsky, Liszt, Gliere, Weinberger, etc. from 7:30 until 11:00. After about eight hours of sleep I picked up the Wind Ensemble again at 10:00 on Monday morning and recorded another fours hours as follows: Khachaturian's ARMENIAN DANCES, Persichetti's SIXTH SYMPHONY, Walter Hartley's CONCERTO FOR 23 WINDS, and HILL SONG NO. 2. I finished your orchestral pieces and the rest of the standard encores the following day from 10:00 A.M. to 2:00 P.M.

Mr. Percy Grainger
Page Two
May 20, 1959

The weeks leading up to this were equally mad but now I am relaxing with equal zeal. By now I trust you have packed your cases and are already on the beautiful UNITED STATES and I trust that this letter will reach you soon. Just as soon as you return to the States in the Fall, we must have a get-together again. Do stay well and mind the dampness! Take care of yourself in all ways and come back to us soon.

The Fennell edition of the Firebird Suite available from Ludwig Music Publishing Company as heard on the Tokyo Kosei Wind Orchestra recording.

I hope we will have done your incomparable music some worthy service this past year. Love to Ella and safe journeys.

Affectionately,

Frederick Fennell,
Conductor

FF:mg

I have all of your music loaned to me wrapped. Shall I keep it here until you return to The States?

ff

Letter from FF to Grainger about the recording of Hill Song No. 2 and eleven other orchestral pieces

3.

They, too, wanted everybody in the audience to know how great is your Posy. I played it there because I wanted all to know what they had been missing all of these years. The Wind Ensemble did play most magnificently and when we were finished, the audience of about 5,000 music educators tendered them an 8 minute ovation.

Heinsheimer told me that they had imported 50 sets of Posy and that lot will go quickly I know.

The recording of Hill Song #2 should be out this week in the album Diverse Winds MG 50221 and as soon as I get copies I will see that you have one. It is an appealing and warmly loving performance by the players who truly loved recording it. Your wonderfully personal note arrived in time to ——— such makes all we do just that much more warm and direct.

We must plan a special observance of your up-coming Birthday! With the eleven orchestral pieces, The Posy, and Hill Song #2 we have stock for record programs all over the country. I am planning to put together a program which I will choose from our recordings and about which I will comment on tape and make available as a package to radio stations.

Are the manuscripts of all of your things securely deposited in your Museum or someplace of similar significance? I surely hope so; for these are treasures and must be thus regarded. Our own Sibley Library should have long ago asked you for anything you might care to give, for it is a great library and worthy of your manuscripts.

I trust that you are well and that Ella too is as busy as ever. I'll be down to see you at Easter time. With all affection and with boundless thanks and admiration.

lovingly Frederick

2 April 1960

Letter from FF to Grainger about recordings.
Courtesy of the Library of Congress.

```
                THE UNIVERSITY OF ROCHESTER
                  EASTMAN SCHOOL OF MUSIC
                    ROCHESTER 4, NEW YORK

                                          April 7, 1960

Mr. Percy Grainger
7 Cromwell Place
White Plains, New York

Dear Percy:

Your three letters (March 22, April 1, April 3) have brightened my days so
illuminatingly. Do continue to take best of care. You were so right not to
attempt a bus ride away from your doctors. By now you should have the monau-
ral copy of HILL SONG #2 I sent you on Monday and I am so overjoyed that you
liked the stereo copy you and Ella heard at the Liberty Shop. I knew how much
this work means to you when I was re-studying it and preparing it for record-
ing. Perhaps some of your love for it crept into my study and our recording --
at least I would hope so. Your admiration for the performance is a great in-
spiration to me and I shall have a long way to go to feel that I have really
done your music the honest justice that it deserves from anybody who conducts.

I know from my wonderful conversations with you that day I came to White
Plains how much you feel that the young years were the best for you as a
composer, and I would disagree only to the extent that you are an eternally
young musical spirit that has always been there just for the beholding -- and
blindness has robbed so many of the beauties. Most of that blindness is
conductor-blindness and with us all this is quite an affliction.

Mr. Wade Pogue's address is Spring Branch Independent School District, 9000
Westview Drive, Houston 24, Texas. I think the idea of your sending photos
to them would be simply marvellous, for they all sincerely were honored to
pen you a line. When you autograph the photo to James Austin, remember that
he was my first trumpet player for three years in the Wind Ensemble and it was
he who blew all that beautiful stuff for you and me in the POSY and HILL SONG
#2 and in seven of our recordings. He is now in Stokowski's Houston Symphony
and teaches at the University of Houston.

Just mail the batch of photos to Mr. Pogue. I will have written that they
should be on the look for them.

Heinsheimer should have ordered 400 sets of the POSY. I could sell that many
myself! I received the letter from your curator and I must send another letter
in terms of that station for there is much I must ask him.

Do continue to write me at 150 Commodore for it is my great anticipation to see
that characteristic hand on the envelope when I come home to Dorothy and Cathy.

Is it possible that I could secure a duplicate copy of your revisions and the
version in E major of COLONIAL SONG that I recorded? I can't find the E major
anyplace and the additions you made in the parts are something I should always
have when I play it with orchestra. No fuss, please -- I just want your best,


Mr. Percy Grainger
Page Two
April 7, 1960

and thanks for the COLONIAL SONG quote in your hand of 3 April. It is such
a lovely spot in a completely lovely piece of music. I will read your appro-
bations to the Wind Ensemble at tomorrow's rehearsal.

Walter Hartley is indeed a gifted man. He wrote me that he thought your HILL
SONG #2 your greatest piece and reminded me that you were his first composition
teacher at Interlochen! (1944)

                                          All the best,

                                          Frederick Fennell,
                                          Conductor
```

Letter from FF to Grainger about the release of the recording of Hill Song No. 2.
Courtesy of the Library of Congress.

Reissues of the of orginal Eastman Wind Ensemble recordings by Mercury.
Courtesy of Polygram Universal.

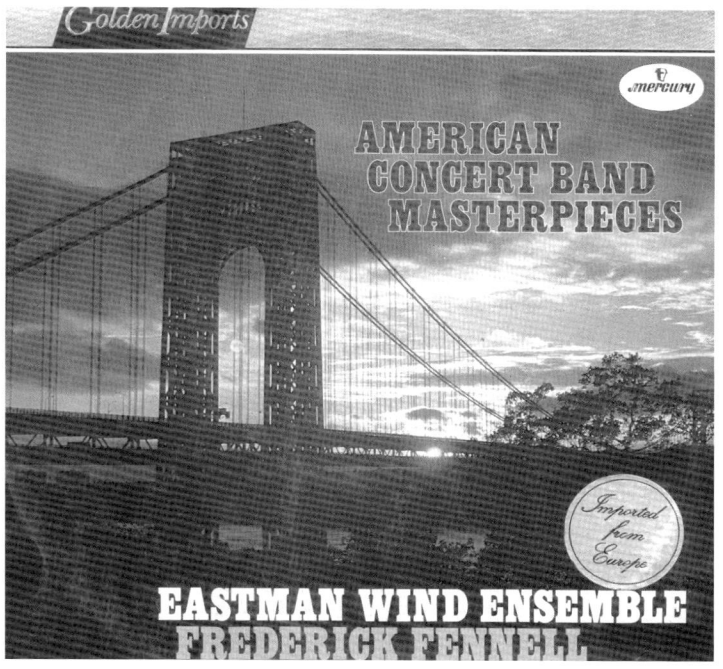

Dear Rob/

Chris at Ludwig sent me your No III of Percy – and what a Beautiful edition it is. I do hope that the profession will embrace it as is their duty beholding the presentation of Who it is!!

As it is – and as I wrote "I never saw a bad Photograph of Percy Grainger." And obviously neither have you.

When someone like him knew who he was and spent his life reaching out to all who would grab his brass ring and have the ride of their life.

Those five lines and four spaces of the many he filled with his exact thought and feeling keep coming back to me – almost as though he felt hemmed in by them, too. So we all keep penetrating. Maybe someday I will have heaved my own heart into a performance – not yet done – "of that night in Rufford Park"! I keep feeling that this is PAG all the way – nobody could get himself so all cranked up! – and that unfortunately is our fault. He beckoned..... and we'd better get in line.

Best to you and your wonderful family.

ff 3/18/03

Dear ROB/ Chris at Ludwig sent me your No III of Percy – and what a Beautiful edition it is. I do hope that the profession will embrace it as is their duty Beholding the presentation of Who it is!! As it is – and as I wrote "I never saw a Bad Photograph of Percy Grainger." And obviously neither have you. When someone like him knew who he was and spent his life reaching out to all who would grab his Brass Ring and have the ride of their life. Those five lines and four spaces of the many he filled with his exact thought and feeling keep coming Back to me – almost as though he felt hemmed in By Them, too. So we all keep penetrating. Maybe someday I will have cheaved my own heart into a performance – not yet done – of "that night in Rufford Park"! I keep feeling that this is PAG all the way – nobody could get him self so all Cranked up! – and that unfortunately is our fault. He Beckoned...and we'd Better get in line. Best to you and your wonderful family.

FREDERICK FENNELL ff 03.18.03

A letter from FF to Rob Simon about the release of the third edition of Percy Grainger: The Pictorial Biography. *This is just an example of the voluminous letters of encouragement Frederick has written to countless souls over the decades.*

Sarah and Rob Simon at a reception honoring the Maestro.

His expressions say it all!
Dallas Wind Symphony, courtesy of Kevin Reed.

His expressions say it all!
Dallas Wind Symphony, courtesy of Kevin Reed.

FF signing a program for one of his fans in Dallas, photo courtesy of Kevin Reed.

A page of manuscript form FF's Library of Congress publication of Sousa's
The Stars and Stripes Forever. How many times has FF performed this piece?
Courtesy of the Library of Congress.

Autobiographical Writing
Frederick Fennell: Lifetime Listener

At a recent press interview an excited young lady asked, "What's it really like up there on the podium making all that music?" The question lit up my flashers: "Deny, deny, deny." The denial was for her last four words, ". . .making all that music?" The first eleven, though equally difficult to really answer, do elicit a positive – if highly personal – response. But those four final ones – they may have hung a colleague or two, I fear, inasmuch as it has been my lifetime belief that "up on the podium" I don't make anything; I just try to listen and react. When it comes to making music the program to be played is the only thing that a conductor can do alone, and that is done out of the listening experience that covers one's conscious lifetime.

Mine probably began at age six when I became aware of my father and his brothers-in-law playing together as fifers and drummers in our family's fife and drum corps. This was part of the annual day-long celebration of the Fourth of July held at Camp Zeke, which was assembled on the two-and-a-half acres that remained of my grandfather's pioneer farm in what is now southeast Cleveland. Describing my family's pursuit of the study of our country's history through these summer-long assemblies at Camp Zeke is even more difficult than replying to my interviewer's so well-meant question about conducting. May it suffice to say that 66 years later I have not yet recovered from the wonderful sounds of those shrieking fifes and rattling drums. They really got my attention, and later when Father hung a very big drum around my very little neck and told me to "play along," I did what I did by listening to what was happening around me. There was nothing very different about that, but I knew from then that this was to be my number-one way to learn while staying out of trouble.

But just avoiding problems is hardly fit behavior for a would-be conductor; I ran headlong into a full catalog of them. My first group experiences came at Miles Elementary School just across the street from where Camp Zeke ended. At Miles my days of playing mostly without music ended when I was introduced to the *Bennett Band Book*

and the *Fox Orchestra Folio*. Then a very cute girl pianist in my classroom and I were asked to play a march out in the big main corridor for the changing of classes. In addition to noticing her, I discovered that we sounded louder out in that cold-looking open space than when we practiced on the warm, carpeted stage in the auditorium. Acoustics began to be part of my listening life along with *Our Director* and Evelyn Bittner, the pianist. Our romance ended a year later when she refused to learn *El Capitan*, but I'm still chasing acoustics and listening to marches by John Philip Sousa.

Next came my first set of drums as a Christmas present when I was ten. My sister Marjorie and I put together another piano and drums act that we played for parties at the mill where our father worked almost all of his life. Our musical inclinations and nature's priceless gifts of hearing and retention came from him. When my father was our age there were no musical opportunities such as his interest and support made possible for us to enjoy at home and in school. Home included a 1926 state-of-the-art phonograph and cabinet filled with a variety of records, and that phonograph's rewarding instant replay set me on my way to begin learning how to listen to music.

The family library included Arthur Conan Doyle's remarkable *Adventures*, and it was while reading one of Sherlock Holmes' recapitulations of how he solved a case by observation and deductive reasoning that I began to apply the Doyle/Holmes words to discipline to become a true listener. The great detective's companion, Dr. Watson, full of questions when expressing amazement at how Sherlock Holmes had discovered the facts that revealed the criminal, would be chided: "My dear Watson, you see, but you don't observe." So too, the musician who hears but somehow forgets to listen, passes rich opportunities to learn.

High school began in the ninth grade when I went to John Adams. There I met a teacher who would further sharpen my listening habits while introducing me to the ordered study of harmonic practice. John B. Elliot's position on the Adams faculty reflected the unusual commitment of the Cleveland Board of Education to the teaching of music; he was our full-time professional accompanist for everything that happened in school. He also taught a class in theory, counterpoint, form and analysis, and music materials, which functioned in tandem with Amos Wesler's orchestra and band rehearsals; it was no surprise when both ensembles became national champions. For those who could meet his high standards, Elliot's classes were a learning experience I could only wish to pass to others; they were to ease me into the next school in my life.

In my high school freshman year Elliot led us through the most detailed and rewarding examination of the *Prelude to Die Meistersinger*, required music for the Greater Cleveland Contest. I still have that miniature score. From it I began the habit of playing while trying to listen for everything – which in *Meistersinger*, of course, is everything. Repeated rehearsals afforded me the chance to isolate instruments. As a challenge I would follow each instrument in a single line of counterpoint or play the game of switching concentration from one to another on call. I had heard a lot of music prior to this but now I was really beginning to LISTEN! – and to think about what I was hearing. *Meistersinger* became my bible of music composition. Elliot's classes, Wesler's rehearsals, and Wagner's music were exciting lessons for a young man.

There were other lessons for those of us in the Cleveland schools at this time; Music Supervisor Russell V. Morgan had worked out a Saturday morning plan of instruction with members of the Cleveland Orchestra and other musicians in the city whereby we could have top teaching for 50 cents a private lesson given in a centrally located school. Cleveland was truly a hotbed of young musical talent in those years. Families who had recently arrived in the United States had produced first-generation children who were to have everything that might have been denied their parents, including the time to practice the violin every day after school. As I participated, I also learned to listen with them.

Listening to the radio was another of my pastimes. One Sunday afternoon in the summer of 1930, I happened to hear a concert broadcast from Interlochen, Michigan played by the National High School Orchestra. It was a shatteringly wonderful experience and I became determined to get to that camp, however impossible it seemed in the second year of the economic depression. Once again the Cleveland schools helped me, this time when I received a booklet about Interlochen from my mentor, Mr. Morgan. When the camp was short on percussion players for the 1931 session, my talented father found the way to get me there. I date my life from those eight weeks spent between the beautiful lakes in the northwestern Michigan woods.

At Interlochen all my listening and studying and practicing were up for grabs. I found myself in company with a stageful of what had to be some of the most outstanding young musicians of that time. The Interlochen Bowl stage, a magic place for so many of us campers, afforded me the next dimensions in my quest for the education I needed to become a conductor. Here I was listening again, with an added ingredient called competition, that dominant element in the world of professional music making. I'm glad I had to face it at this early age when I was just beginning to learn a few things about myself. Fellow percussionists, older and with two summers of camp experiences ahead of me, were way out in front. Listening as I watched them play, I began to close the gap of experience between us.

I was never without a pair of heavy drum sticks under the belt on my blue corduroys, a rubber practice pad in one hip pocket, and a dog-eared miniature score in the other. (I didn't need a pitch-pipe for tuning the kettledrums; I just listened to the one nature had put in my head.) The summer was spent listening and sopping up everything I heard at Interlochen.

Placement of percussion instruments (and especially the kettledrums) in large ensembles offers a panoramic view of the technical command of the conductor as well as all that is happening in the other sections. Usually it is while listening from the rear (where balance is easily disturbed) that percussion players lose touch with what is happening in front of them. The percussion part is a problem, for it rarely tells players anything beyond when to play; even how to play and with what is vague. The good percussionist is thereby obliged to become an acutely tuned listener and to develop retentive habits that account for all that is played. Listening while following the score or a violin or clarinet part is much more informative and rewarding than trying to be an adding machine. Listening to the sonorities of which the percussionist's music is part is the key to balance and the only reliable guide to texture. At camp I had the chance to do this twice daily seven days a week. I had not been there long before my principal concern was to find some way to get back there for my two remaining years of high school.

It was interesting to discover that first summer that retentive listening saved me a lot of time and that it wasn't just the music I could remember. The visual scene of the trees in the grove, the hour of the day with the morning aroma of the canvas awning in front of the bowl being heated by the sun, the look of a Breitkopf & Härtel music cover, the smell of the pines, the way horn players in front of me barely got the tuning slides back in place to play after dumping water – all these are still indelible memories of the first time I played Brahms' *Symphony in C Minor*. All these sensory receptions and retentions were stimulated by listening as I heard.

I did make it back to camp the next two summers and was fortunate to add two more disciplines to the experience of performing. The urge to conduct had been fed a bit the first summer when Vladimir Bakalienikoff herded about 50 of us into Grunow Hall for his basic class in baton technique. Knowing that anything beyond that class was strictly daydreaming, I took the only route open to me in 1932 as a potential music leader – the Interlochen course in drum majoring, all 5'1" of me! Mr. Giddings, Director of Instruction, arranged for me to attend the university class, Drum Majoring and Field Tactics, offered by Mark H. Hindsley, whose pioneering Cleveland Heights High Marching Band was peerless on the field. His order and logic in teaching those studies were in sharp contrast to the guarded secrets of the twirling baton when I sought some lessons from a counselor at Boys' Camp. The counselor told me that, in the best tradition of the magician, I could keep what I could steal from him – which I did.

Returning home to my final fall at John Adams I found Mr. Wesler open to the idea that I might be the band's drum major. At least and at last I could conduct the band for marching although that square one-two, up-down motion didn't really interest me, even then. My life as a music leader was happening and I have always cherished the way it began; the long road to a podium was to be shortened considerably by events that occurred in the summer and fall of 1932.

It was time to be thinking about a music school, like the one in Rochester, New York, where Dr. Howard Hanson was director. We all knew him as annual guest conductor of the National High School Orchestra; and his school had everything I needed, including a generous program of student financial aid. We had talked about it in 1932, but there was no action on my application for admission as late as June of the following year. William F. Ludwig, Jr. became a camper in 1932, and by 1933 we were close friends and sharing the kettledrum stool on a draw lots basis. Bill drew the lot for Dr. Hanson's visit that year. Desperate to make any points with Hanson, I was grateful when Bill offered me his week so that I could play in Hanson's first Interlochen performance of Symphony No. 2, "Romantic." This is probably how I became a percussion major at Eastman that September; Interlochen's fork in the road pointed straight to Rochester, New York.

The discipline I chose for my final high school camp session was composition. Among the pieces, I wrote for class was a mildly successful march. I decided at camp, however, that I would neither clutter nor pollute the world with further creative attempts and that I would devote my life to listening and hopefully to conducting the music of others. This, too, was a listening decision made by all that great music from the *National Emblem* to *The Rite of Spring*. Before this abandonment, however, Dr. A. A. Harding had invited me to make my debut as a conductor with the National High School Band leading that summer's march composition at the final concert. A treasured photograph of the occasion reveals all that could possibly be wrong in a very young conductor – except the look on my face.

At Eastman, as at Interlochen, I was free of the usual domestic responsibilities – no trash to take out, no grass to cut, no wood to carry for Grandma Putnam's magic oven (but no pies and cakes, either). Listening was for keeps at Eastman, where amidst the fast pace I was oh-so-grateful for all to which I had been exposed en route.

If memory is born of interest and listening is fed by curiosity, why not pool all of these as we listen to others perform, practice, rehearse, improvise, warm-up and down, wherever and whenever we find them? I was about to learn some of these big lessons if hardly all the answers.

I had never seen a real chamber music hall, let alone one as strikingly beautiful as Kilbourn, or a theater as impressive as the one that bore the name of George Eastman. Word was that this genius of industry and finance with an obvious passion for music could not (perhaps to his eternal regret) carry a tune in a basket. Maybe this is why he built and endowed so magnificent a school for the training of those who could. Both of these remarkable halls were to become important rooms in my life. Everything about the Eastman Theatre was impressive – the sheer size, the beautiful murals, the elegant crystal chandelier, the big stage – but the setting was not what struck me then. What made me stop and pay attention was the sound of that marvelous acoustical chamber, which later was to become so vital a part of the many phonograph recordings that the Eastman Wind Ensemble and I would make there.

The first time I heard the special sound of that theatre I was in it all alone – which I never should have been. Over the years the never-should-have-beens were to mount; but for now they were confined to surreptitious forays into the darkened Eastman Theatre, where in the silence of those ghostly surroundings I could listen to the thoughts in my head.

The preliminaries accomplished, I spent those first weeks at school adding to life's two inevitables, death and taxes, a third called theory – thank you, John Elliot. We music students knew we were in a school of a university where the academics took no secondary place. The parent University of Rochester recently had moved to a beautiful new campus where its College for Men was housed. An aerial photo showed a modest but handsome athletic stadium with high stands on one side. I thought I'd try becoming involved as drum major with whatever football and marching band activities there were. I asked the director of athletics at the River Campus (who also had the challenging responsibility for teaching Eastman's most hilarious class, hygiene) if he could tell me where I might contact the leader of the band for an audition as drum major. His reply that they didn't have either lit up all my youthful flashers and this time the printout was: go, go, go! "How would you like to have a marching band, Dr. Fauver?" I asked. "I can organize and lead one for you." After a silence, which I was fortunate not to break, an unforgettable look of disbelief crossed his face. Two weeks later, however, when several willing sources of energy pooled their resources into a group – many former Interlochen campers joining out of courtesy, other people out of curiosity – Dr. Fauver's look of approval was unhesitating.

It was a pretty good parade – thank you, Mark Hindsley. My career as a band conductor had begun as an Eastman School freshman with no warning of its arrival and no hint of the consequences ahead. While the money I earned put me through school, the audacity of my act put me in touch with kindred souls, and I had a great need for both. The number one kindred soul and critic (I needed that, too) eventually became my wife after a succession of bone-chilling fall Saturday afternoons and all that attends life with the conductor of a marching band. Dorothy Codner didn't much care for bands as she heard them, and some of the time neither did I. Doing what we could about that was to consume much of our life together. A violinist who switched to viola, Dorothy was a year ahead of me in school. I was happy to have found myself through her.

School was tough. In addition to old-fashioned competition came grades, class lessons, studio pressure, practice-room checkers, and house mothers. Eastman had been around for 11 years and Howard Hanson had been its director for almost all of them; there was no doubt of his complete (but benevolent) authority and the students' great admiration for his musical leadership. My little bit of business with Dr. Fauver and the assembling of those never-should-have-been marching Eastmanites (plus men from the college which paid the bills) happened only with his approval.

Eastman's resources reached beyond practice rooms and marble halls into immediate and intimate association with the thriving professional music life of the city of Rochester, located right across the corridor from the school. The professional life was always part of our education, and non-university groups shared the rehearsal and performance facilities so generously provided by Mr. Eastman. The chance to hear our teachers play for keeps under almost every imaginable ensemble circumstance, six days a week, was the ultimate lesson. Furthermore, when it became apparent that the skills our teachers demanded in the studio were the same ones they needed under the pressure in the professional hall, it encouraged all of us to reach beyond what we had thought was our potential. This lesson, together with the immense holdings in the Sibley Music Library, were Eastman's greatest assets.

After the initial success of the band that marched while it played, some of the players encouraged me to organize one that sat down in a nice, warm room. The University of Rochester Symphony Band played its first concert on January 25, 1935, on campus. It was my debut conducting a concert band. Howard Hanson was present and requested a repeat performance a few weeks later in Kilbourn Hall. When the dust had settled our name was changed to the Eastman School Symphony Band, and we were added to the ensemble curriculum. I was the group's conductor for the next 26 years.

Our percussion teacher and performer par excellence, William G. Street, was a solid supporter of my moves toward conducting. At the same time I was still a percussionist, and I practiced the instruments as though that was all I had to do. I performed in all the school's ensembles, and when I graduated with my class in June 1937, I was Eastman's first percussion major to receive the Performer's Certificate.

Bill Street had taken me into the section of the Rochester Philharmonic a few years before. It was an opportunity of priceless value for a young conductor to be part of a group with such a high level of professional playing and to be in the company of international soloists. There was much for which to listen, and I had scores to everything that I could buy of what was played.

The music director of the Philharmonic was the distinguished Spanish musician and pianist, Jose Iturbi, who enjoyed the privilege of parking his car in the garage under the main rehearsal room. Hearing sounds from above, he came upstairs unobserved to watch a rehearsal that I was conducting with the band. Some days later, to my complete surprise, he asked me to conduct a portion of the same work, Enesco's *Rumanian Rhapsody,* so that he might go out into the Eastman Theatre to hear the Philharmonic's sound and balance. Hearing the wonderful sound of the Orchestra coming right at me, so well-played and so responsive to whatever I did, was overwhelming. I began to feel what it was like to be up there on the podium "making all that music."

My first employment was not as a conductor but as a kettledrummer with the San Diego Symphony Orchestra. I was hired to play the full 1936 summer season at

The Bowl in Balboa Park as part of the California-Pacific International Exposition. Others from Eastman, including two players who had gone to San Diego High School with the conductor, Nino Marcelli, were in the orchestra as well. The cross-country trip in my car, mostly alone, was an education in itself. I'd never seen an ocean, and my first view of the Pacific coming up over the brow of a hill in what is now Camp Pendleton was a sight that has never left me. California was very different from New York; San Diego was charming and beautiful. Rehearsing and playing daily in a good orchestra became another way to expand my knowledge of repertory and learn what worked. Playing from scores and listening for everything was endlessly informative.

That summer, Otto Klemperer, conductor of the Los Angeles Philharmonic, offered a cycle of the Beethoven symphonies on Monday nights at the Hollywood Bowl. We San Diego players had the night off, so in company with Norman Herzberg, our first bassoonist, and Harold Kurtz, the flutist who had steered us into the San Diego job, and I drove to Hollywood to hear performances of those masterworks. Seated on the fringe of the sound in the Bowl I heard things that I still associate with the proper interpretation of this literature. The lack of amplification did not seem to hinder the strength of the music. Klemperer was impressive, not only as a conductor, but also as one so tall that he did not need to use a podium.

One Monday afternoon the San Diego's wind players and I went neither to the bathing cove at LaJolla nor to Klemperer's Beethoven. Instead, John Barrows, our principal hornist, assembled us at his family home, a classic California wooden cottage with ample room and a great sound for chamber music. Among the works to be read was a piece I had not heard, the *Serenade*, Op. 7, by Richard Strauss. I was along as a listener, but when things became a little rocky in the middle section (B minor, *piu animato*) Herzberg suggested that I assist the ensemble. The subsequent play through was the beginning of a long love affair with this charming piece; I had found one of the pivotal scores that would lead me to the Eastman Wind Ensemble. At summer's end Norman and I went to see the Big Trees at Yosemite; at last they were more than just black-and-white photos in a geography book.

School and the marching band season began without Dorothy, who had graduated and returned home to Iowa. In 1935 the University of Rochester had a new young President, and somewhere among the myriad questions asked him was one by a local sports writer as to when the band might get some real uniforms. His casual reply that an amount would be allotted for the fall of 1937 was enough encouragement for me to request a cost quote from Greenville, Illinois. The quote led to drawings and a fitting session for all the men who would return. With the slim assurance of a few devoted alumni that somehow the bill would be paid, I gulped a few times and sent in the order. Two weeks later I hurried off to Iowa to be married. The automobile trip to San Diego and the 1937 summer season of the San Diego Symphony were our honeymoon. Back in Rochester, the new uniforms had arrived, along with a huge bill. I went to see President Valentine, the bill in my hand and my job on the line. Somehow, and with his appreciation of what the band had been contributing, another never-should-have-been came to pass.

Both Dorothy and I were in graduate school on a very tight budget – hers! We practically lived in Sibley Library, researching our material for dissertations in music theory. *The Orchestral Development of the Kettledrum from Purcell through Beethoven* demanded and got every other minute of my time for two years; the rest of my work went on around it. I became a looker as well as a listener. Research to support the thesis meant that I had to explore all printed scores before Purcell and then patiently to peruse every score in the complete works of Purcell, Bach, Handel, Haydn, Mozart, and Beethoven. Through this survey of a composer's use of the kettledrums I had the chance to observe much beyond that area as well.

School had barely begun that fall of 1937 when a notice appeared on the bulletin board from the Institute of International Education advising that applications for the Salzburg International Prize in Conducting should be completed by the first of October. The Mozarteum in Austria would award the prize the following summer. This was the only prize for a young conductor at the time, but confidence that my training and experience made me eligible was tempered by a realization that conductors of bands sat rather low on the artistic totem pole. I vividly remember dropping that application in the Eastman corridor mailbox and thinking, "Well, who knows?" Howard Hanson, Jose Iturbi, and Vladimir Bakaleinikoff had agreed to let me list them as sponsors; when time passed with no acknowledgement, I finally ceased to think about it. The mountain of paper on my Sibley study cubicle received all of my attention. On the 28th of February word came that I had been awarded the prize after a jury had secretly visited the darkened Eastman Theatre during a Symphony Band rehearsal.

Dorothy's and my happiness at this great opportunity ended as abruptly as it had begun with the news on March 12 that Hitler had completed the annexation of Austria for the Third Reich. Wanting no gifts from Nazism, I relinquished the prize, and my disappointment was eased when the Mozarteum Academy's summer plans were cancelled. Dorothy and I were in Iowa for the summer when I received a telegram from Howard Hanson stating that the prize was on again. The State Department requested that I please be in Salzburg by July 10th. Somehow I was, and alone. The sudden change from pastoral Iowa to the busy decks of the German liner *Europa* found me with my nose once again in a German dictionary.

The first night in Salzburg I lodged in a comfortable private home. The score to Mozart's *Jupiter* rested atop a great white down comforter as I read my way into the spirit of my new surroundings. Amid reflections of the family, teachers, and players who had sent me there, sleep was about to claim me when I heard the distant but unmistakable sound of marching boots approaching in a precise crescendo. Then this rude interruption of Mozart and my reverie became the accompaniment to German soldier songs. As the marchers sang and passed, sleep no longer came easily or peacefully. I knew that evening in Mozart's beautiful hometown, as a wonderful time was beginning for me, that things were about to go all wrong for lots of other people; those boots in the night were just an omen of its beginning.

Growing as a Conductor

Salzburg was unlike any place I had seen before, and it started my imagination working overtime. Walking down the streets where Wolfgang Amadeus had gone before, my feet never touched the cobblestones. The Mozarteum Prize that had brought me to the city offered daily seminars in score study together with the usual student postmortems of the previous night's opera or concert and a few brief visits with Wilhelm Fürtwangler, the Festival's chief conductor. My day-to-day instruction came from Herbert Albert, chief at the Opera in Stuttgart. Just being that close to the Vienna Philharmonic was a daily lecture in a style of orchestral playing that had helped to set standards for the world. The Mozart orchestra provided playing sessions for the class. On these occasions my Symphony Band podium experience rewarded me with the honors position at our final concert when Albert thought it was appropriate that I should conduct the "Scherzo" and "Finale" of Dvořák's *New World Symphony*.

Studying at the Mozarteum was a pleasant and encouraging confirmation of my musical talents. It provided exposure to a different language, to another culture with its museums, libraries, theaters, and restaurants. Most important of all, however, was the adjustment of my conductorial alignment to include the orchestra. The mere physical act of having proceeded up and down gangplanks that connected the United States to Europe and back again framing brief residence in a name European conservatory certified me as a bona fide conductor. Just to prove the point, I had been back in Rochester for only three weeks when my brothers in Alpha Nu chapter, Phi Mu Alpha Sinfonia Fraternity invited me to become conductor of their superb Little Symphony.

Eastman's growing popularity with ever-better players emerging from the high schools had swelled the size of Symphony Band to overflowing. I searched for quality transcriptions, and even harder for anything original. Unlike a typical college, university, or conservatory band, we had no uniform, no budget, no officers, no organization – just Dorothy, me, and one vastly underpaid library assistant. The simple words of Director Howard Hanson guided the instrumentation: ". . .if your applied music is not strings, but an orchestral or band instrument, you will play in Symphony Band."

The result was an ensemble that grew in size because of the popularity of such teachers as Emory Remington and Joseph Mariano whose students in the 1940 Band numbered 14 trombones and baritones, and 14 flutes. The Eastman Theatre stage was filled by an additional 6 oboes, 2 English horns, 4 bassoons and contra, 12 horns, 10 trumpets, 5 tubas, 2 string contrabasses, 2 harps, and 5 percussion; total: 98.

I considered the group to be just an overgrown wind quintet, whose purpose was to provide an additional ensemble experience in basic repertory regardless of how far the music might be wrenched from its original key and orchestration. Style is style; all the elements of nuance and dynamic were there to be achieved as faithfully as possible.

This pursuit was a training course for me that I never could have found elsewhere. I wanted to conduct, and with Symphony Band I was able to start at the beginning – by learning how to rehearse. I'd had the experiences all of us do as we learn to play an instrument in a group, and remembering both the good and the not-so-good of them was a solid base for my beginning hours on the podium. The listening habits I had developed when I was a player were just the training I needed to be conducting this group. Those games I had played at isolating instrumental textures and switching contrapuntal lines were probably what kept me up there on the podium.

I learned all my lessons there, on the hot box. In the first years two-thirds of the band were upperclassmen. They met me more than halfway; I just kept things moving so there was no time for problems. I knew that I must always come thoroughly prepared for every aspect of the rehearsal. If anything, I probably came over-prepared at first, but with friendly counseling I gradually learned how to pace my plan as the rehearsal unfolded. There were times, amidst tension and stress, when I had to remind myself that trying to be a conductor had been my idea. Nobody, except my half-frozen marching band friends seeking a nice, warm room had invited me to do this.

I knew that I needed to develop my own technique and in the process, I stood in the shoes of many a famous maestro of my youth. Most of them were comfortable, to a certain extent, but when I began to feel the pinch I knew they weren't my shoes. Remembering what did feel comfortable, I would slip into Toscanini's or Stokowski's for a while. Faculty colleagues, beginning with Dr. Hanson, never hesitated to tell me what was working and what techniques they thought I should get rid of. The criticisms I treasured most were from my wife, Dorothy, who had seen and heard it all.

For the summer of 1939, my master's degree behind me, Joe Maddy invited me to join the faculty at Interlochen as teacher of percussion. Working in the first of the buildings given by the Ludwigs was my final commitment as a percussionist. That summer brought me a close friendship with another man whose absorption with music would bring and keep us together for years. At the time Oscar Zimmerman played on the principal stand of string contrabasses in Arturo Toscanini's NBC Symphony. As an encore to his serious solo bass recital (rare in those days), he asked me to join him in a surprise presentation of Bob Haggart and Ray Baduc's popular novelty for bass and jazz drums, The Big Noise from Winnetka. That was the first jazz ever played at Interlochen Bowl and it was a sensation. If I had to draw the double-bar on my career as a percussionist, that was the way to go. "The Big Noise" didn't cause any damage either; the next summer Maddy and Giddings made me conductor of the National High School Band.

Dorothy spent the summer of 1940 as a member of Leopold Stokowski's All American Youth Orchestra, and it served both her and me, for her letters were filled with keen observations of Stokowski's superb technique and his imaginative concepts of orchestral playing. I studied him carefully for several months and his beautiful suede shoes felt very comfortable. Friends who played in the Little Symphony urged me to try to get into Serge Koussevitzky's class at a new summer Music Center called Tanglewood. I relinquished the Interlochen post when he invited me to come in 1942.

My stay at the Berkshire Music Center began with an outdoor reception at which I met my colleagues in the class, Robert Zeller, Walter Hendl, Lukas Foss, and Leonard Bernstein. Lenny was in his third summer there, and from observing as he coached in the open theater, a great career for him seemed inevitable.

Serge Koussevitzky was a remarkable man. His annual visit to Rochester with the Boston Symphony always guaranteed a brilliant and precise performance, and from my vantage point as an usher in the balcony of the Eastman Theatre, his conducting had an air of mystery enhanced with elegance. Koussevitzky's technical approach was almost diametrically opposite that of Toscanini's, whose rapier-like baton left nothing in doubt. Koussevitzky's stick was not much longer than an unsharpened pencil, and it fit the rest of him perfectly. Both he and Toscanini were slight in physical stature, and both of these great men wore superbly tailored clothing that elevated them as they stood on the podium "making all that music." However different Koussevitzky's approach may have been from Toscanini's, they arrived at the same destination: making great music.

"Koussey," as we called him behind his back, was a great teacher. He had the ability to find simple ways for us to develop the resources within each of us. We were not to imitate others, beginning with him. I didn't need to slip into his shoes, because he quickly convinced me that my own fit much better. It was fun to discover myself again.

Koussevitzky's English was colorful and highly personal, charged with elements from other languages he spoke. Words were unimportant in the exultation of music that exuded from his every pore. Koussevitzky gave unstintingly of himself, his knowledge, and his experience. He also taught entrance, exit, bowing, dressing, tea drinking, and manners.

Haydn's 88th *Symphony in G* was my first assignment with orchestra at Tanglewood. The first movement passed without comment; as I began the second Koussevitzky came up to the stand and as the music died he quietly said, "Too slow – remember two things, first to sing it, then to bow it and always listen to the orchestra." The admonitions were not forgotten.

We got along very well and when Tanglewood resumed after World War II he invited me to be his assistant with the class and to conduct one of the orchestras; unfortunately, Tanglewood was closing down for the duration. Four years previously while I was so busy living Act II of *Der Freischutz* the big decisions leading to the war were being made in Berchtesgaden, not many kilometers down the road from the Mozarteum. Those Salzburg boots in the night had caught up with all of us.

It was no surprise to be turned down by already overstaffed Washington service bands and no disappointment, either, for I wanted to be a fly-boy. They told me to go home; I was an old man–at age 29. One particularly gloomy November morning Hanson called to ask me to meet a man who had a proposition that might interest me. The head of National U.S.O. music stateside had come to Rochester to attend the funeral of composer Nathaniel Dett, composer of *Juba Dance*, who had died on United Service Organization assignment; and on Armistice Day I took my oath to serve the U.S.O. as his replacement. Dorothy had to stay in Rochester because of her orchestra contract.

The trip from Chicago to San Francisco took an incredible five days. Not knowing I had pneumonia, I was shipped south to San Diego. I arrived in Los Angeles in a coma and was carried to the hotel listed on the itinerary in my pocket. When I failed to keep a date with Eastman organist Catherine Crozier Gleason, she called the hotel and I woke up eight days later in the critical ward of Los Angeles County General Hospital with Jose Iturbi sitting beside the bed. He took care of my release. A huge depression followed, and the only things keeping me on course were a small radio and my miniature score to *Tristan und Isolde*.

After a reunion with Dorothy at Christmas we wound up in San Diego where the U.S.O. had on its hands 76 units of the major services in San Diego County. At once I found myself with armored forces training in the desert. With my ukulele and harmonica I was to lead the G.I.s in community singing. The holes they stared through me made them my toughest audiences, ever.

In San Diego, the great Navy town, that service was my primary concern. At my desk a Captain whose salt-encrusted braid was his identification introduced himself, laid $10,000 on my blotter, and asked if I could find him a piano. The U.S.O. did not accept such funds and by that time there were no pianos at any price. He wanted it for his C.V.E.; the money had come from the bar and soda fountain for the officers who flew from the deck of his carrier. Another such visitor had brought his buglemaster (C.V.E.s were not authorized for musicians); they wanted manuscript paper and band instruments in any state of disrepair. They had some funds with which we wheedled two tired clarinets and so-so cornets from the last store with anything to sell. They took trash from the repair bins, a badly mashed old helicon tuba, and a C melody sax that had been on a top shelf for years. Somehow in the aircraft maintenance shops the musicians made the instruments work and put together a band of 10 players. When they sailed from North Island, their band played an *Anchors Aweigh* I shall not forget.

Then there were all those wonderful musicians who had enlisted in the bands. I had not been in San Diego very long before Navy Musician Robert Marsteller suggested the great potential of a U.S.O. evening during the week when musicians in service could adjust their pass/liberty time to come and play just for the fun of performing the music they knew before the war. Bob had been one of those marching Eastmanites and he knew how to spread the word around the Navy installations. I found the music in the Clark Collection at the Los Angeles Public Library and got clearance to use the Roosevelt Junior High band room. The first rehearsal was an absolute joy for about 50 players from all services. We just read the tunes down, one after another, no rehearsing. Missing instruments were quickly covered by doublers. We later turned a vacant Masonic Lodge room into a rehearsal hall with practice rooms, listening booths with records, and a small library of chamber music. When a concert benefiting Russian War Relief was held, Jose Iturbi volunteered to play the Grieg *Concerto*. We were a smash. The correct description of my position was: civilian music officer, no rank, pins, stripes, or benefits; but the work gave me access to many places and people that U.S.O. might serve.

Suddenly the war was over and the streets were filled with celebrating people. Back in Rochester, school was already jammed with former students and lots of new faces. It didn't take long to sense that many things had changed. The innocent sequence from high school to college had been interrupted by the war. G.I.s sought to be excused from the band because they'd ". . . had three years of it!" We had to make the G.I. Bill work to serve those students.

A new item on my agenda was the College Band Directors National Association, which became a necessary seminar on the many post-war problems that musical ensembles faced. Preparation for the annual conferences and my own problems where none had existed before raised serious questions with no easy answers. Out of frustration, I suggested to the wind and percussion faculty that we regroup the players into orchestral wind sections. My associates didn't like that idea, but I did extract from them a promise to clear the one o'clock hour for miscellaneous wind groups.

The Little Symphony appointment, Salzburg, and maturity – together with a lot of just plain listening – had opened my view of wind repertory training for Eastman students. Endless digging in the Sibley stacks revealed fresh treasures waiting to be performed. Our one o'clock rehearsals finally led to a 1951 concert in Kilbourn Hall that engaged almost every wind music major in the school. We played the following works:

- *Ricercare for Wind Instruments, Willaert*
- *Canzon for Wind Instruments, Scheidt*
- *Motet: Tui Sunt Coeli for Brasses, Lasso*
- *Sonata pian e forte, Gabrieli*
- *Canzon Noni Toni a 12, Gabrieli*
- *Suite No. 2 for Brass Instruments, Petzel*
- *Three Equale for Trombones, Beethoven*
- *Serenade No. 10 in B♭ for Winds, Mozart*
- *Serenade in E♭ for Winds, R. Strauss*
- *Angels, for Brasses, Ruggles*
- *Symphonies of Wind Instruments, Stravinsky*

I included scholarly comments about the music as part of the invitation to attend. The success of this informative departure from customary concerts at school prompted plans for another performance in 1952.

The bottom dropped out when it was discovered in November 1951 that I was seriously infected with hepatitis. Weeks in a hospital were followed by more at home. The only prescription for recovery was absolute rest, a pound of sugar candy with gallons of water daily, and a strict diet. I had not had a real vacation since I was a boy, and meditation wasn't part of those jam packed Eastman days and nights. Because I was under orders to barely move my eyeballs, I decided to make the most of all that time on my back.

The Kilbourn concert had convinced me that we needed a reed, brass, percussion, and keyboard ensemble with a fresh point of view and a name that could start from its own square one. With nothing to do but suck lemon drops, drink water, and stare at the ceiling, I had plenty of time to bounce around my thoughts about this wind group, some of which dated back about 20 years. Recall was easy in all that solitude, so I reached back to conversations with fellow campers, among them one with Sidney Mear, as good a cornet player as any I knew in 1933. Walking back to Boys Camp through the Interlochen woods I had asked him how he liked sitting first chair in such a fine big band with so good a conductor as Dr. Harding. Allowing it to be okay, he had added that one thing bothered him: "Anytime I want to put my horn down I can hear 10 other guys playing my part." The 10 would have to go. I wanted a carefully balanced instrumentation capable of performing styles from 16th-century brass music and moderate-sized chamber music to Paul Hindemith's new Symphony in B♭.

Using the basic format of the British military band but increasing it to allow for triples among the reeds required for Stravinsky's Symphonies, each player would be the soloist his private teacher always taught him to be. I had never met anybody who taught "section clarinet" so we could cut the players to one on a part allowing for divisi.

I could hear how clean this sound was going to be, for I knew it from the orchestra; but now I could apply that attitude and its clarity to band music. We would sit in the straight rows of orchestral seating. While we were at it, why not make some reference recordings of the best of the band's music, since none existed? I was supposed to be at absolute rest, and I was, except for the fact that I had been told of the high fatality rate of people in my condition. What worried me most was that I might forget some of what I had planned before I was well enough to sit up and write it all down. Then Dorothy brought me a notebook into which I wrote what I had bounced off the ceiling about what I had decided to call a wind ensemble. Now I really had to get out of that hospital where the daily blood test called the tune.

One afternoon a concerned Dr. Hanson came to see me. Conversation with him was always inspiring. He was about to leave when he asked if there was anything he could do for me. "Yes, Dr. Hanson, since you ask, there is," I said. "Here in this bed I've had the chance to think through a plan for a new wind group for school, which I hope you'll consider letting me try." I gave him my notes and he sat down to read them. After a while his hand moved involuntarily for the inevitable cigar. When he smiled and began to make those familiar little conducting motions with the still-unwrapped panatela, I knew I had his attention. The Eastman Wind Ensemble played its first rehearsal on September 20, 1952.

1986, 1987 © The Instrumentalist Company, Reprinted with permission.

The Library of Congress Historical Publication of The Stars and Stripes Forever by John Philip Sousa with notes and additions by Frederick Fennell and Jon Newsom. Courtesy of the Library of Congress.

Honors & Awards of FF

1929 .... Wins a contest for a trip to Washington, D.C. to meet for 20 minutes with President Hoover. FF enthusiastically sold the most tickets for a Marine Band Concert to win this trip. Little did he know he would conduct the Marine Band 69 years later.

1931 .... Scholarship to attend the National Music Camp at Interlochen, Michigan.

1932 .... Awarded special recognition of Scholarship by John Adams High School.

1933 .... Graduates from John Adams High School in Cleveland, Ohio.

Attends the Eastman School of Music at the University of Rochester on a music scholarship.

1937 .... Earns a Bachelor of Music Degree in percussion and music theory. FF is the first Eastman graduate to earn a degree in percussion.

Awarded a fellowship to the Salzburg Mozarteum in Germany to study conducting with Wilhelm Fürtwangler. This was the only conducting Award available to young conductors in the 1930s.

1939 .... Master of Music Theory from the Eastman school. Becomes a member of the Eastman conducting faculty.

1942 .... Invited to the Tanglewood class of Serge Koussevitzky. Classmates included Lukas Foss, Walter Hendl and Leonard Bernstein.

1952 .... Conducts at Yaddo Music Festival.

Creates the Eastman Wind Ensemble.

1950-1960s ..... Records 22 albums in high-fidelity for Mercury Records.

1954 .... *Time and the Winds* by FF published by LeBlanc.

1958 .... Honorary Doctorate in Music from the Oklahoma City University.

1961 .... Receives a citation and a medal from the Congressional Committee for the Centennial of the Civil War for two volumes of recordings of the Music of the Civil War.

Recording of Music of the Civil War earns a Grammy Award for music and gunfire.

1962 .... Associate conductor of the Minneapolis Symphony.

1964 .... Recruited to the University of Miami at Coral Gables, FL.

1960s .... Honorary chief in the Kiowa tribe.

Fellow in the Company of Military Historians.

Member in the Society of the Sons of the American Revolution.

1969 .... Recipient of the 25th Anniversary of Columbia Ditson Conductor's Award.

1970 .... Recipient of the New England Conservatory's Symphonic Wind Ensemble Citation.

Honors & Awards of FF

1970 .... Awarded the Gold Record Award from the Mercury Record Corporation.

1975 .... Awarded the Arts Oscar from the National Academy of Wind and Percussion Arts Association.

1977 .... Eastman School of Music Alumni Citation for the 25th Anniversary of the founding of the Eastman Wind Ensemble.

Fennell's recording of Grainger's *Lincolnshire Posy* with the Eastman Wind Ensemble is selected by *Stereo Review* as one of the "fifty best recordings of the Centenary of the phonograph 1877-1977."

Named to the Board of the Scala Memorial Fund Library of Congress.

1981 .... Awarded the University of Rochester Outstanding Alumni Award.

1982 .... Receives the Kappa Kappa Psi Distinguished Service Medal.

1984 .... Starts guest conducting the Tokyo Kosei Wind Orchestra.

1985 .... Presented the Star of the Order from the John Philip Sousa Memorial Foundation.

1988 .... Receives Honorary Doctorate from the University of Rochester.

1989 .... Receives Interlochen Medal of Honor.

Midwest International Band and Orchestra Medal of Honor.

1990 .... Inducted into the National Bandmasters Association Hall of Fame.

1991 .... Becomes the first recipient of the Medal of the International Percy Grainger Society for Distinguished Services.

FF and TOKWO receive the first Bandmasters Academic Society of Japan Award for Outstanding Musical Performance

1992 .... Frederick Fennell Hall is dedicated in Kofu, Japan, with a TOKWO concert on July 17, 1992.

Named Laureate Conductor of the Tokyo Kosei Wind Orchestra.

1993 .... Bio-Discography *ffortissimo* is published by Ludwig Music - written by Roger E. Rickson.

1994 .... Receives the Theodore Thomas Award of the Conductors Guild, Inc., in recognition of unparalleled leadership and service to musical performances throughout the world. The previous two recipients of this award were Maestros Leonard Bernstein and Georg Solti.

1996 .... "Listen" a printed documentary is published about FF by Kosei Publishing, Japan.

1998 .... First civilian to conduct the "Presidents Own" United States Marine Band.

2001 .... Inducted into the American Classic Music Hall of Fame.

2002 .... FF publication *Time and the Winds* is re-released.

2004 .... Receives the first Lifetime Achievement Award from the Piedmont Wind Symphony and the North Carolina Music Educators Association.

Index

Akiyama, Toshio 178
Anderson, Leroy 10, 52-53
Asbury, Wayne 127

Badolato, Jim 86
Battisti, Frank 110, 128, 132
Beck, Dennis 144; John 48; John R. 143
Benjamin, Barry 76, 77
Berliner, Jay 86, 87
Bernstein, Leonard 10, 18, 41, 134, 231, 236, 237
Bigelow, Ralph 155
Bishop, Ronald 80
Bobo, Roger 83, 89
Bookspan, Michael 136
Bostley, Ed 8
Broun, Ronald 184
Buckley, Condr. Lewis J. 165

Camp Zeke 14-15, 17, 84, 222
Carey, Tanya Lesinsky 66
Champouillon, David 165
Chelengarian-Greene, Helen 131
Chevallard, Lt. Colonel Philip C. 164
Cleveland Winds 29, 130-131, 133, 135
Cliburn, Van 99, 185
Copland, Aaron 10, 41, 50, 103, 106, 145
Coppen, David Peter 89-90
Cozart, Wilma 67, 210

Dhus, Earle 121
Doherty, Lynne 28
Donze, Chris 186-187

Edgar, Paul F. 106-107

Faulhaber, Michael 40
Fennell, Dorothy Codner 18, 28, 31, 38, 40, 226, 228-231, 234
Fetter, David 76, 200
Fillmore, Henry 10, 80, 85
Fine, Robert 25, 52, 67
Flesher, Sandy 70, 168, 200
Foley, Colonel Timothy 166
Foss, Lukas 10, 18, 41, 231, 236
Fricano, Sam 48, 50
Friedman, Ron 122
Fürtwangler, Wilhelm 10, 18, 229, 236

Giddings, Thaddeus P. 15, 225, 230
Ginther, Dr. John 143
Gonano, Max 7
Grainger, Percy Aldridge 7-11, 13, 25, 27, 29, 32, 53, 87, 94, 130, 133, 142, 154, 184, 208, 210, 211, 214, 216, 237

Hall, David 52, 122, 137
Hamilton, John 7
Hanson, Howard 10, 15, 17, 21-22, 40, 66, 78, 94, 96-97, 121, 155, 225-231, 234
Harding, Albert Austin 15, 20, 225, 233
Hayasi, Yasuro 181
Hill Song No. 2 7
Hoffman, Richard 62
Holst, Gustav 7, 10, 11, 13, 27, 38
Hurlburt, Jeannette Dowd 42, 127

Inglefield, Kenley 56
Instrumentalist 7, 8, 25, 28, 30, 36, 50, 128, 153, 234

Interlochen 5, 10, 15, 17-19, 21-22, 28-31, 33, 35-38, 40, 42, 53, 70, 73, 78-79, 83, 111, 113, 120-121, 126, 127, 128, 164, 225-226, 231, 233, 236-237

Janis, Byron 105
Johnson, Cliff 131
Jones, Brian 134
Julian, Jonathan 197, Linda 197
Junkin, Jerry 188

Kawamura 5-6, 12, 107, 139-140, 146, 148-150, 153, 160, 169, 171, 173-175
King, Karl 10, 29, 80, 184
Klinger, William 104
Knaub, Donald 56
Kosei Publishing 5-6, 12, 107, 139-140, 148-150, 153, 160, 169-171, 173-175, 178-181, 237
Koussevitzky, Serge 10, 18, 41, 231, 236
Krance, John 10, 100

Lawrence, Harold 67, 200
Lee, William F. 28, 102-103, 106
Lincolnshire Posy 8, 10, 27, 29, 142, 209, 237
Linssen, Dries 159
Lister-Sink, Barbara 154
Ludwig, Elizabeth 9, 29, 32, 36, 68, 142-143, 147, 154, 168, 184, 186, 200; William F., Jr. 21-22, 35, 85, 88, 225
Lutz, Anne 125

Maddy, Joseph 15, 31, 38, 230

Index

Manville, Stewart 7, 154
Martin, Jennifer 133
Mastroianni, Roger 80, 202, 204
McKee, Max 147
Mentzer, Dr. Thomas L. 124
Milhaud, Darius 27, 39
Miller, Tom 56
Mitchell, Gilbert 142
Miura, Toru 133, 178

Neidig, Kenneth L. 36-38
Newman, William S. 7
Newsom, Jon 13-15, 17, 19, 29, 32, 114-115
Niwano, Nichiko 178
Nowak, Hank 147
Ouzer, Louis 47, 49, 55, 57-61, 63, 64, 65, 66, 67, 69, 71, 77, 116-117, 123, 152, 155-157

Parker, Bob 106
Parkman, Paul D. 124
Patterson, Vincent 141
Peters, Gordon 69
Phillips, Harvey G. 112
Pick, Kenneth 125
Pierce, Gregor 136
Poccia, Nicholas 45
Preucil, Doris 54

Reed, Alfred 106, 117-118; David 7; Kevin 188-191, 195-196, 217-219
Remington, Emory 56, 230
Renshaw, Jeffrey 132, 152

Robinson, Angela Decarne 45

Schissel, Loras John 41, 182, 202, 205
Schweikert, Norman 50, 53
Seiffert, Stephen 70, 73
Severinsen, Doc 28, 102
Shanly, Gretel Y. 61
Sheldon, Robert E. 70, 83, 85, 94-95, 97, 114-115, 168, 200-202
Sherman, Roger 77
Shirley, Wayne D. 8
Simon, Robert 10, 11, 154, 184-185, 202, 216, 220
Slocum, Earl 162
Street, William G. 17, 227

Telarc 7, 28, 129-133, 135
Tokyo Kosei Wind Orchestra 28-29, 138, 141-142, 145, 158, 170, 187, 213, 237
Tucker, Patrick 197

Ussachevsky, Vladimir 155

Vaughan Williams, Ralph 7, 10-11, 13, 25, 27, 130

Whitney, John 128
Whitwell, Sir David 117
Wickstrom, Fred 102-103
Wilder, Alec 10, 74-75, 112
Williams, Clifton 103, 106
Winer, David 132

Yaddo Music Group 206, 236

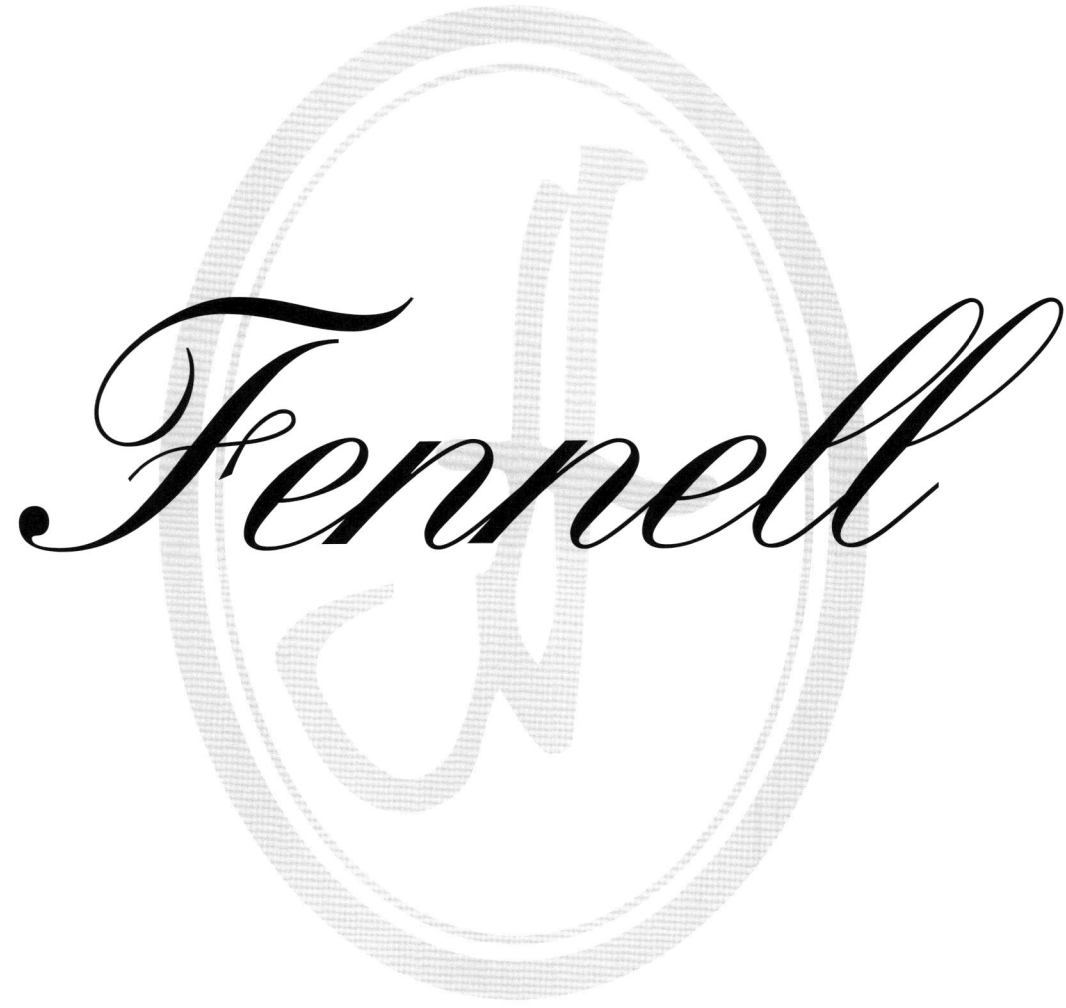
Fennell